Fitness Matters addresses five key areas of fitness fit and healthy throughout your lifetime:

- Cardio-Respiratory Fitness
- Muscle Strength
- Muscle Flexibility
- Core Stability
- Healthy Eating

Fitness Matters is a series of manuals giving practical advice on how to:

- Sustain a fit and healthy heart through regular daily cardio-respiratory exercise.
- Keep strong using free-weights.
- Improve joint mobility and flexibility in the muscles and tendons.
- Develop good core stability using the inflatable ball and doing basic abdominal and back exercises.

It is essential to develop and maintain strength in the skeletal muscles as well as in the core group of muscles, such as the abdominals, to facilitate good posture. It is equally important to keep as mobile and flexible as possible as well as keeping the heart and lungs in a fit and healthy condition. Combining regular exercise with a balanced healthy diet is the way to control and maintain your weight and body fat levels within the recommended range appropriate to your height, age and gender.

The healthy heart manual also provides essential information about good nutrition to help keep you fit for activities for daily living, as well as the nutritional requirements for those of you who are more seriously involved in sport.

Fitness Matters to the young as they develop physically. **Fitness Matters** to middle-age people to ensure they keep fit and healthy for their working years and leisure pursuits. **Fitness Matters** to the elderly to help them stay healthy, active and enjoy their later years of life.

Fitness Matters to the population of the UK and worldwide to overcome the consequences of inactivity and unhealthy eating habits which can arise as a result of a modern lifestyle and advancing technology.

Make **Fitness Matter** to you by being active on a regular basis and eating healthily.

CHARTEX

A SERIES OF FITNESS MATTERS

STRENGTH TRAINING

STRENGTH TRAINING

Strength training involves a muscle or group of muscles working against a resistance resulting in an increase in tension in the muscle fibres. In ancient Greek times it is said that Milo of Croton trained by carrying a newborn calf on his back until it was fully-grown. As the calf got heavier he got stronger. Thus as you increase the Intensity, (resistance) the Duration, (number of repetitions you perform at each exercise) and the Frequency (how often you train each week) of training, so does the strength of the muscle and muscle group gradually and progressively overload the musculo-skeletal system resulting in it becoming stronger.

There are two main types of muscle contraction, which will influence the development of strength. When a muscle shortens or lengthens during its contraction to move a limb through a full range of motion the contraction is **"Isotonic"** whereas **"Isometric"** type of strength training involves contraction of muscle without any change in the angle of the joint when working against a resistance.

The exercises in this manual involve **isotonic muscle contraction** where the weight (resistance) is constant. However, there are considerable changes in muscle tension during the isotonic contraction because the angle of the joint varies during the lifting/pushing or pulling action involved in the exercise. This affects the force which the muscles need to make when performing a resistance movement, as there is a weak joint position at some point during the full range of motion. It is at this point when the muscle needs to work harder than at any other time during the exercise.

Without becoming too technical for this instruction manual it is worth understanding the difference between concentric and eccentric muscle contractions when working in isotonic training. When a weight is lifted eg Biceps curl (see page 16) the concentric contraction occurs in the muscles that are working against the resistance ie the barbell or dumb-bell. The muscle fibres shorten and become thicker reducing the angle of the joint as the two ends of the muscle which are attached to the bone structure - origin and insertion - come closer together as the weight is lifted to the finish position.

In eccentric contraction the muscle is lengthening as it "pays out" to control the lowering of the weight to the start position. Hence all the instructions alongside the exercise illustrations in the manual tell you to "return under control to the start position."

Working with dumb-bells and barbells and body weight provide the muscles with a "constant resistance" method of strength training where the weight does not change.

BENEFITS OF STRENGTH TRAINING

- Promote and develop greater muscular strength.

- Improve your muscle "tone" which can make you look good, and feel better.

- Improves muscular endurance, which delays the onset of fatigue when playing sport and in activities for daily living.

- It can improve cardiovascular fitness, as there is an increase in the body's basal metabolic rate when there is an increase in muscle mass, which helps to promote fat loss.

- It improves posture, gives better support to the joints and reduces the risk of injury in activities for daily living whilst at work or participating in a leisure pastime.

- It also reduces the likelihood of osteoporosis in women in later life and when linked to an appropriate fitness regime strength improves general health and longevity. Studies have shown that the elderly (70 - 80 year-olds) who begin training with weights have found a marked benefit to their lives.

- Strength training can also help to maintain good flexibility as well as increase the thickness and strength of tendons, ligaments and other connective tissue. This promotes a healthy response to impulses from working muscles and will therefore improve co-ordination of movement.

- Building and maintaining strength throughout the body can help cope with the stresses that both activities of daily living and sport put on the body. Strong legs and strong grip help with "ADL" (Activities for Daily Living) such as lifting and carrying objects. Modern professional and amateur sportsmen and sportswomen benefit in their chosen sport when they do controlled and supervised strength and muscle development. Muscle strength in the lower limbs has a proven effect in providing stability to the knee and ankle joints. Similarly this applies to muscle strength around the shoulder, upper back and upper arm to give stability to the shoulder joint, whilst strength in the abdominals and deep muscles of the back help to maintain the spine in good neutral alignment.

- Weight training exercise can also increase the levels of dopamine and seratonin, which may help deal with mood swings and fight depression.

This Manual provides a comprehensive programme of resistance exercises using dumb-bells and barbells. It also includes a warm-up programme as well as exercises for strengthening abdominal and back muscles. Weight training exercises are approved by B.W.L.A. (British Weight Lifters Association).

PRIINCIPLES
OF STRENGTH
AND
MUSCULAR
ENDURANCE
TRAINING

4

STRENGTH - MUSCULAR ENDURANCE TRAINING

It is important to decide what you are training for, whether it is a particular sport/athletic event or general fitness for an active lifestyle. When training for a particular sport or athletic event your strength training programme will reflect their specific requirements. Therefore it is important you select the exercises, which work the appropriate muscle groups. The body takes time to adapt itself to specific training and so it is advisable to start by developing strength in all the major muscles of the body at the endurance end of the training continuum.

The "Training Continuum" diagram below shows the range of training for the various strength and muscular endurance components of fitness.

TRAINING CONTINUUM

High Reps Low Resistance **Endurance** 25-55% of 1 Rep Max 20-25 Reps/set	Speed of Movement **Power** 60-75% of 1 Rep Max 8-12 Reps/set	Low Reps High Resistance **Strength** 80-95% of 1 Rep Max 4-7 Reps/set

1 Rep Max = Maximum weight lifted once at each exercise.

For muscles to get stronger they must be trained in an overload state and as they adapt to this overload, strength will improve by progressively increasing the resistance which the muscles work against. This principle can be applied to training for muscular endurance, power and muscular strength.

The continuum shows **muscular endurance** at one end involving work against a low resistance as a percentage of the maximum weight you can lift once at each exercise, with a high number of repetitions. This will produce dynamic endurance in muscle by involving the recruitment of more muscle fibres. Increased capillary action results in increased blood flow through the muscles providing them with more oxygen and fuel. It also helps to remove metabolic waste products. This can help to prevent the muscles from tiring whilst at work, playing sport or enjoying other leisure activities such as gardening. This type of training is especially important in later years of life.

PRIINCIPLES
OF STRENGTH
AND
MUSCULAR
ENDURANCE
TRAINING

5

PRINCIPLES OF STRENGTH AND MUSCULAR ENDURANCE TRAINING

At the other end of the continuum is **muscular strength**, which relates to muscles working against a resistance, which requires maximum effort to do the exercise. Training to improve muscular strength involves working against a high resistance with a low number of repetitions. As the resistances are progressively increased so the muscles become stronger.

Training to improve **power** involves **strength with speed** and is an important requirement for many sports and therefore there is a close relationship between strength and power in a training programme.

BEFORE TRAINING FOR POWER IT IS ESSENTIAL TO:

- **Warm-up and stretch properly.**
- **Have a good strength base in all major muscle groups.**
- **Choose exercises that will allow speed of movement and that this explosive action is performed correctly and under control.**
- **Work against a resistance that will allow a fast, controlled movement.**

HOW TO ESTABLISH YOUR STRENGTH TRAINING PROGRAMME

It is important to decide why and what your strength training programme is designed to achieve for example:

a) develop and maintain good muscle tone for an active lifestyle.
b) train for a particular sport.

Whether it is a) or b) it is advisable to start with a programme of exercises that will improve the level of strength throughout the major muscle groups of the body. Working at the endurance end of the training continuum will help the muscles adapt to resistance training and establish a platform on which to build a training programme for general fitness or for more sport specific strength.

Whilst this manual deals with exercises using dumb-bells and barbells, if you visit a gym to train, there is usually a range of weight training machines to use if you wish to vary your exercise programme. However, the principle is the same if you are working on a constant resistance training method. You need to decide the overload, which you are going to work against and therefore you need to assess your absolute strength in the muscle groups at each exercise. This is achieved by performing one repetition at the maximum weight lifted. From this information a strength training programme can be designed involving:

Repetitions – the number of times you perform the exercise

Sets – the number of sets you do which comprise the number of repetitions you do in each set, for example; one set could comprise 15 repetitions; three sets would be written 3 x 15 reps.

Workload – this refers to the resistance which the muscle or muscle group will work against. Below is an example of a schedule for one exercise when training for muscular endurance, power, and absolute strength. Use this principle for each weight resistance exercise.

Training Weight – Endurance 25% of maximum weight lifted.
Power 60% of maximum weight lifted.
Absolute Strength 80% of maximum weight lifted.

Example of Training Ratios				
EXERCISE Barbell Bicep Curl	1 Rep Max Weight	Training Weight	No of Reps	No of Sets
Endurance	40kg	10kg	15 - 20	3
Power	40kg	24kg	8	3
Absolute Strength	40kg	32kg	4 - 6	3

HOW TO ESTABLISH YOUR STRENGTH TRAINING PROGRAMME

Once the muscle group has adapted to the resistance you can increase the weight, increase the repetitions or adjust the number of sets. Refer to the Training Continuum on page 4 to determine how to improve your strength; for example:

Endurance	Weight	Reps	No of Sets
	10kg	18	3

The period of adaptation would depend on how often you train. On average this would be two or three times per week, which allows a rest period of at least 48 hours before the next training session. The effect which training has on the body is shown in the diagram on the next page. Always start your training programme with exercises that train the large muscle groups after you have warmed up properly. Follow the warm-up exercise routine as set out in this manual on pages 10 - 13.

Using free-weights is a very effective and efficient way of developing strength and can be done in the comfort of your home with the appropriate equipment or in a gym environment.

An example of a training programme for muscular endurance:

Exercise	Resistance	Reps	Sets	See Page
1. Dumb-bell Squats	15kg	15	3	30
2. Dumb-bell Bench Press	5kg each Dumb-bell	15	2	21
3. Single Arm Dumb-bell Rowing	5kg	15	2	26
4. Lateral Dumb-bell Raise	3kg	15	3	25
5. Alternate Dumb-bell Biceps Curl	5kg each Dumb-bell	15	2	15
6. Single Arm Triceps Extension with Dumb-bell	3kg	15	2	18
7. Abdominal Exercise Hands to Knees sit up*	Body on floor	15	3	38
8. Back Exercise Shoulder Raise*	Body on floor	15	2	41

Rest for 30 seconds between sets and at least 1 minute between each exercise.
*Abdominal and back exercises are performed at the end of the session because working other large muscle groups first helps to provide a good blood supply to the gut and deep muscles of the spine, which make these exercises easier and safer to do.

N.B.: Cool down properly after training.

TRAINING PROGRESS LADDER CHAREX

THIS DIAGRAM SUMMARIZES WHAT HAPPENS TO THE BODY WHEN YOU TRAIN

STRENGTH
• Able to apply greater force against a resistance and with less effort.
• Increased strength provides a good basis for developing power.

POWER
• Increased capacity to produce explosive and dynamic movements.

INJURY PREVENTION
• Training effects reduce the chances of injury.

IMPROVEMENT IN STRENGTH AND POWER AS THE RESULT OF TRAINING

• Muscle fibres grow (Hypertrophy).
• Toughness of tendons increase.
• Composition of bone becomes stronger.
• Connection between tendon and bone becomes stronger.
• Better and more efficient muscle fibre recruitment.
• Increased capillary network providing greater blood supply to the muscles.
• Increased energy supply.

ADAPTATIONS TO RELIEVE STRESS DURING REST PERIOD FOLLOWING TRAINING, THIS COULD TAKE UP TO 48 HOURS

• This is what happens in the training sessions.

PHYSIOLOGICAL AND METABOLIC STRESS ON THE BODY

STRENGTH AND POWER TRAINING SESSIONS

WARM-UP AND COOL-DOWN EXERCISE ADVICE

Why you should warm up before exercise/training

- It provides the body with a period of adjustment from rest to exercise.
- It improves physical efficiency by raising heart, metabolic and respiratory rates.
- It makes a gradual demand on the circulatory and respiratory systems.
- It increases body temperature; bodily processes are more effective at warmer temperatures.
- It increases muscle temperature; it results in more efficient chemical reactions at higher temperatures.
- It improves circulation; it takes about 3 to 5 minutes to redistribute the blood to the muscles during warm-up.
- It improves oxidative processes; blood gives up the oxygen which it is carrying to the muscles more efficiently as you warm-up.
- It prepares the body for co-ordination of movement related to the requirements of strength training; messages between your brain and muscles are sent more effectively.
- It can reduce the risk of injury. The likelihood of muscle tears, ligament strains and muscle soreness is reduced.

Why you should cool down after exercise/training

- It enables the body to adjust from exercise to rest, lowering the heart rate in a controlled way.
- It helps the body deal with removal of waste products from the muscles during the recovery process and reduce muscle soreness.
- It facilitates muscular relaxation and by stretching helps to prevent muscle shortening.

How to cool down

- Cool down by gradually decreasing the intensity of cardio-respiratory exercise over 6 to 8 minutes.
- Follow this aerobic exercise with stretching exercises that were done in the warm-up.
- Hold each stretch for about 10 - 15 seconds and do a minimum of 2 repetitions at each stretch.

HOW TO WARM UP

- The warm-up should last about 20 minutes.
- It is a combination of intensity and duration without undue fatigue.
- There should be a minimal time lag between warming-up and strength training.
- Monitor your heart rate by taking the radial pulse (on your wrist) or carotid pulse (on your neck), as it is a good indicator of your heart rate. A heart rate monitor is a more reliable method of measuring your heart rate during cardio-respiratory exercise.

PHASE 1: INCREASE BODY AND MUSCLE TEMPERATURE BY DOING APPROXIMATELY 6 MINUTES OF CARDIO-RESPIRATORY EXERCISE.

- It is important to gradually build up the pace and intensity of cardio-respiratory exercise to about 65% of maximum heart rate (MHR). This is calculated by subtracting your age from 220 (i.e. MHR = 220 – age). If you are unfit use 200 instead of 220 to calculate your MHR.

- For example if you are a fit 40 year old:

220 – 40 = 180 x 65% = approximately 120 beats per minute.

However, if you are an unfit 40 year old:

200 – 40 = 160 x 65% = approximately 105 beats per minute.

CHOICE OF CARDIO-RESPIRATORY EXERCISES AT HOME

| Jogging on the spot | Walking to Jogging to easy running around the area where you live | Step-ups – on a step bench or the stair | Knee Raises | Heel Flicks | Skipping |

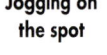      

CHOICE OF CARDIO-RESPIRATORY EXERCISES USING MACHINES

| Exercise Bicycle | Rowing Machine | Stepper | Cross-Trainer | Jogging Treadmill |

HOW TO WARM UP

PHASE 2:
MOBILIZE THE MAJOR JOINTS BY DOING MOBILITY EXERCISES

- Do 5 repetitions of each exercise – working both limbs in each direction.

- Keep a smooth, rhythmical action when doing each movement.

ANKLES
Plantar Flexion   **Dorsi Flexion**   **Eversion**   **Inversion**

KNEES
Knee and Hip Flexion

HIPS
Hip Flexion and Abduction

- Go through all four movements when rotating the ankles.
- Push down, pull up, rotate outwards then inwards.

- Flex the hip as you bring the knee up towards the chest.
- Clasp hands in front of knee to increase flexion.

- Bend the knee up until level with the hip.
- Take the knee up, round to the side and down in a circle movement.

TRUNK
Thoracic Rotation

SHOULDERS
Shoulder Rotation

NECK
Neck Rotation   **Lateral Flexion**

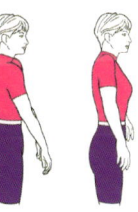

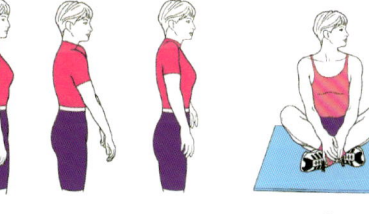

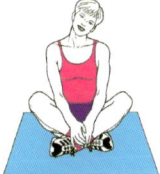

These exercises can be done sitting or standing

- Stand with the feet shoulder width apart.
- Fold arms and raise to shoulder height.
- Rotate the spine in both directions keeping arms at shoulder level, hips facing forwards.

- From a relaxed start position, rotate shoulders, forward, up and back then round to the start position.

- Rotate the head to the left looking behind the shoulder to end range of motion.
- Repeat to other side.

- Tilt head in a lateral movement taking the left ear towards the left shoulder.
- Repeat to other side.

PHASE 3:
STRETCH
THE MAJOR
MUSCLE
GROUPS

12

STRETCH MAJOR MUSCLE GROUPS

HOW TO WARM UP

PHASE 3:
STRETCH THE MAJOR MUSCLE GROUPS

- Hold stretches for about 6 - 8 seconds.

- Do a minimum of 2 repetitions for each stretch.

- Work systematically through the body to ensure that the main muscles and tendons are stretched properly.

Soleus Stretch
(Calf Muscle)

Stretching Technique
- Use arms for support and stability.
- Place leg back. Bend knee, keep foot flat, heel down and toes pointed forward.
- Push knee forward over foot keeping hips in line with shoulders.

Gastrocnemius Stretch
(Calf Muscle)

Stretching Technique
- Use arms for support and stability.
- Keep leg straight, foot flat, heel down and toes pointed forward, (avoid locking knee).
- Lean whole body towards wall from the ankle, keeping hips in line with shoulders.

Hamstring Stretch
(Back of Thighs)

Stretching Technique
- Bend forward from the hips, keeping the spine in natural position.
- Bring the foot up to a neutral position as the stretch is held.

Quads Stretch
(Front of Thighs)

Stretching Technique
- Using arm for support.
- Bend knee, grasp ankle from behind with same hand.
- Pull leg backwards from the hip keeping knees together.
- Avoid leaning forward, tilt pelvis slightly backwards.

Adductor Stretch
(Inside of Thighs)

Stretching Technique
- Stand in a straddle position.
- Slowly bend left knee keeping it aligned over the foot.
- Keep right foot flat and rotated outward to approximately 45°.
- Avoid inward rotation of knees.
- Keep shoulders in line with hips to avoid leaning forwards.

HOW TO WARM UP

Lumbar Spine and Gluteals Stretch
(Lower Back and Hips)

Stretching Technique
- Sit with left leg fully extended, ankle pulled up towards you.
- Cross right leg over left leg to stretch the right hip.
- Rotate spine to right as left elbow crosses right knee.
- Keep shoulders relaxed while supporting body with right arm directly behind right hip.

Lower Back Stretch

Stretching Technique
- Lie on the back on a firm surface with legs bent, feet flat on the floor.
- Bring each leg upward one at a time and grasp behind the knee.
- Pull both knees together towards the chest.
- Keep shoulders relaxed.

Cat Stretch
(Spine)

Stretching Technique
- Kneel on all fours, with hands shoulder width apart and knees hip width apart.
- Tighten abdominals, inhale and arch back.
- Progress this action from lumbar and thoracic through to the cervical spine.
- Relax the head at end of sequence.

Lateral Flexion of Spine

Stretching Technique
- Stand with feet slightly turned out shoulder width apart.
- Extend the right arm up towards the ear.
- Lean to the left side with shoulders relaxed, spine and head kept in a neutral position.
- Avoid spinal rotation and lateral hip movement.

Posterior Shoulder Stretch
(Back of Shoulder)

Stretching Technique
- In a standing position raise arms to shoulder level.
- Grasp arm above right elbow with left hand.
- Slowly pull arm across chest without rotating shoulders or trunk.
- Maintain head in a neutral position.

Anterior Shoulder/Chest Stretch
(Front of Shoulder)

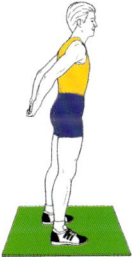

Stretching Technique
- Clasp hands together behind back, depress the shoulders.
- Extend both arms back and upward to end range of motion whilst maintaining an upright position.
- Maintain head in a neutral position.

Triceps Stretch
(Back of Upper Arm)

Stretching Technique
- Bring right arm up and behind head.
- Grasp right elbow with left hand, press back and downward, taking the right hand down the back.
- Maintain the head in neutral position.

NOW START YOUR TRAINING/EXERCISE SESSION

DUMD-BELL AND BARBELL CHARTEX

DUMB-BELL AND BARBELL WEIGHT TRAINING EXERCISES

Approved by B.W.L.A. (British Weight Lifters Association)

Elbow Flexors and Forearm Muscles

Triceps and Forearm Muscles

Chest and Shoulder Muscles

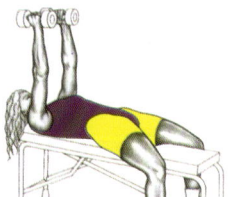

**Shoulders, Upper Arm
and Upper Back Muscles**

Leg Muscles

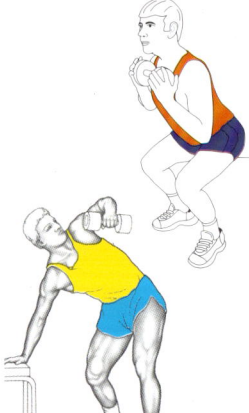

Leg and Trunk Muscles

PLUS

Abdominals and Back Exercises

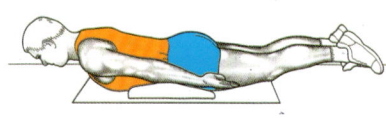

EXERCISES FOR ELBOW FLEXORS AND FOREARM MUSCLES

MAJOR MUSCLES WORKING

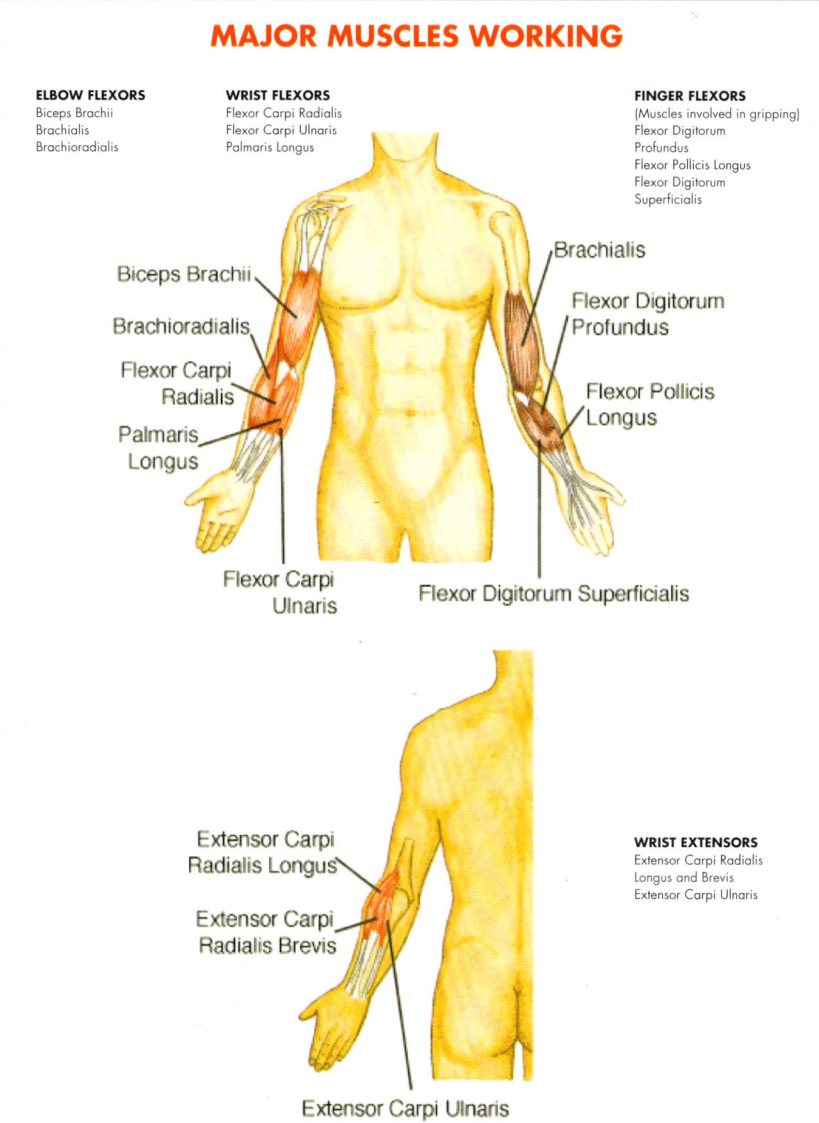

ELBOW FLEXORS
Biceps Brachii
Brachialis
Brachioradialis

WRIST FLEXORS
Flexor Carpi Radialis
Flexor Carpi Ulnaris
Palmaris Longus

FINGER FLEXORS
(Muscles involved in gripping)
Flexor Digitorum
Profundus
Flexor Pollicis Longus
Flexor Digitorum
Superficialis

Biceps Brachii
Brachioradialis
Flexor Carpi Radialis
Palmaris Longus
Flexor Carpi Ulnaris

Brachialis
Flexor Digitorum Profundus
Flexor Pollicis Longus
Flexor Digitorum Superficialis

Extensor Carpi Radialis Longus
Extensor Carpi Radialis Brevis
Extensor Carpi Ulnaris

WRIST EXTENSORS
Extensor Carpi Radialis
Longus and Brevis
Extensor Carpi Ulnaris

GENERAL SAFETY INSTRUCTIONS
• Check all equipment before use.
• Place feet slightly wider than hip width apart to provide a firm and well balanced base.
• In all exercises lower weight to start position under control.
• Maintain appropriate stability and correct technique as shown.

BREATHING
• Breathing should be rhythmical during each repetition.
• Breathe IN on the effort.
• Breathe OUT as you return to start position.

ELBOW FLEXORS AND FOREARMS
CHARTEX

DUMB-BELL EXERCISES

1 ALTERNATE DUMB-BELL BICEPS CURL

Major Muscles Working:
Brachialis, Biceps Brachii, Muscles involved in gripping.
Forearm Muscles work to stabilize the Wrist.

- With an alternating sequence, curl and lower dumb-bells under control, keeping elbows into your side.

- Straighten each arm when returning under control to the start position.

- Breathe freely during the exercise.

START POSITION

2 DUMB-BELL SCREW CURL

Major Muscles Working:
Brachioradialis, Biceps Brachii, Brachialis, Muscles involved in gripping, Supinator and Forearm Muscles work to stabilize the Wrist.

- Grasp dumb-bells with knuckles facing outwards.

- Rotate dumb-bells bringing knuckles to face forwards as you raise the dumb-bells up to the shoulders to the finish position.

- Return under control to start position.

START POSITION

3 BENT FORWARD DUMB-BELL CURL

Major Muscles Working:
Brachialis, Biceps Brachii, Muscles involved in gripping, Forearm Muscles work to stabilize the Wrist.

- Place feet wider than hip width apart.

- Keep back straight with head up.

- Raise dumb-bells up to shoulder level keeping elbows close to knees.

- Return under control to start position.

- Elbow flexors will work harder during this exercise.

THIS IS AN ADVANCED EXERCISE

START POSITION

BARBELL EXERCISES
ALL THESE EXERCISES CAN ALSO BE DONE WITH DUMB-BELLS

**Major Muscles Working
in these three exercises:**
Biceps Brachii, Brachialis, Brachioradialis, Wrist Flexors
and Extensors, Muscles involved in gripping.

4 STANDING BICEPS CURL

START POSITION

- Grasp bar with hands shoulder width apart, palms facing forwards.

- Keep elbows free at side of body, back straight and knees slightly bent during the exercise.

- Keep the bar close to the body and the elbows behind line of bar throughout the movement as you bring the bar up towards the shoulders.

- Return under control to start position.

5 REVERSE BICEPS CURL

START POSITION

- Grasp barbell with hands shoulder width apart, knuckles facing forwards.

- Bring the bar up towards the shoulders.

- This is primarily a wrist and forearm exercise working the wrist extensors and, therefore, a very firm grip is required.

- Keep the back straight and knees slightly bent during the exercise.

- Return under control to start position.

6 BARBELL WRIST CURL

START POSITION

- Keep elbows firmly in contact with the bench and maintain a firm grip on the bar throughout the exercise.

- Keep the back straight as you curl the bar up.

- Return under control to start position.

TRICEPS AND FOREARM

EXERCISES FOR TRICEPS AND FOREARM MUSCLES

MAJOR MUSCLES WORKING

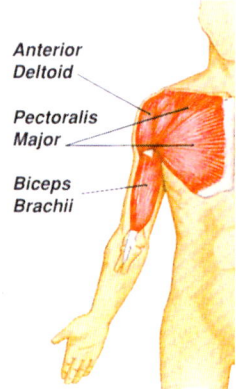

Anterior
Deltoid

Pectoralis
Major

Biceps
Brachii

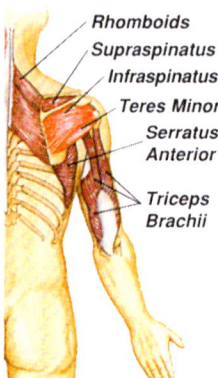

Rhomboids
Supraspinatus
Infraspinatus
Teres Minor
Serratus
Anterior
Triceps
Brachii

WRIST EXTENSORS
Extensor Carpi Radialis
Longus and Brevis
Extensor Carpi Ulnaris

ELBOW EXTENSORS
Triceps Brachii
Anconeus

WRIST FLEXORS
Flexor Carpi Radialis
Flexor Carpi Ulnaris
Palmaris Longus

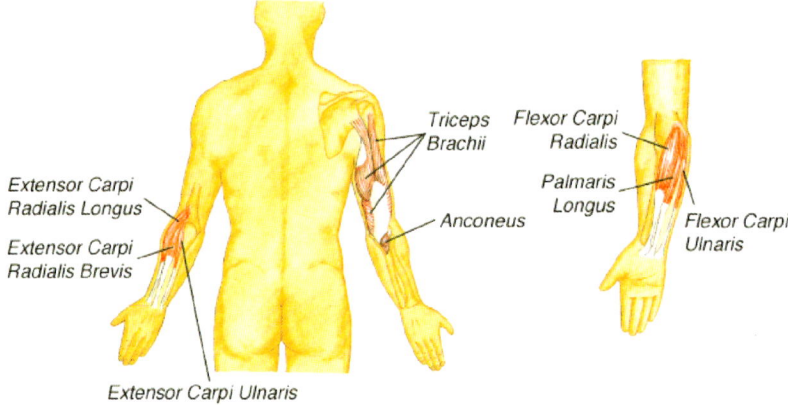

Extensor Carpi
Radialis Longus

Extensor Carpi
Radialis Brevis

Extensor Carpi Ulnaris

Triceps
Brachii

Anconeus

Flexor Carpi
Radialis

Palmaris
Longus

Flexor Carpi
Ulnaris

GENERAL SAFETY INSTRUCTIONS
- Check all equipment before use.
- Place feet slightly wider than hip width apart to provide a firm and well balanced base.
- In all exercises lower weight or body to start position under control. Keep the body still and maintain correct technique as shown.

BREATHING
- Breathing should be rhythmical during each repetition.
- Breathe IN on the effort.
- Breathe OUT as you return to start position.
- For DIPPING – Breathe IN as you lower and OUT as you thrust upwards.

DUMB-BELL EXERCISES

**Major Muscles Working
in the first three exercises:**

Triceps, Anconeus, Wrist and Forearm Muscles.

1 DUMB-BELL TRICEPS EXTENSION

- Stand with feet slightly wider than hip width apart.

- Keep body erect and upper arm in vertical position at side of head.

- Fully straighten the elbow to take dumb-bell above the head.

- Return under control to start position.

- Exercise both arms.

START POSITION

2 SINGLE ARM TRICEPS EXTENSION

- Use a bench or chair for support.

- Keep upper arm firmly against side of body when extending the elbow.

- Keep back straight and head up, and take upper arm to a horizontal position as shown.

- Return under control to start position.

- Exercise both arms.

START POSITION

3 BENT FORWARD TRICEPS EXTENSION (KICK BACKS)

- Keep upper arms firmly against side of body when extending the elbows.

- Keep back straight and head up, and upper arms in a horizontal position as shown.

- Return under control to start position.

START POSITION

CHARTEX

TRICEPS AND FOREARM

BARBELL AND BODY WEIGHT EXERCISES

4 CLOSE GRIP STANDING TRICEPS EXERCISE

START POSITION

Major Muscles Working
Triceps, Anconeus, Deltoid, Muscles involved in gripping.

• Grasp bar with hands approximately 6" apart and bring it up to rest on the back of the shoulders.

• Keep body erect and elbows high.

• Straighten the arms to finish with the bar above the head. Return to start position under control.

5 REVERSE DIPPING

START POSITION

Major Muscles Working
Triceps, Deltoid, Teres Major.

• Assume start position then lower body down under control until elbows are at right angles as shown.

• Thrust up from this position to extend the arms back to the start position.

6 CLOSE HANDS PRESS-UP

START POSITION

Major Muscles Working
Triceps, Pectoralis Major, Anconeus, Deltoid and Trunk Muscles.

• Support the body with feet hip width apart and hands less than shoulder width apart.

• Keep body straight and head up.

• Lower hips and chest to touch the floor.

• Press-up to the start position.

MAJOR MUSCLES WORKING

ELBOW FLEXORS
Biceps Brachii
Brachialis
Brachioradialis

WRIST FLEXORS
Flexor Carpi Radialis
Flexor Carpi Ulnaris
Palmaris Longus

FINGER FLEXORS
(Muscles involved in gripping)
Flexor Digitorum
Profundus
Flexor Pollicis Longus
Flexor Digitorum
Superficialis

Biceps Brachii

Brachioradialis

Flexor Carpi
Radialis

Palmaris
Longus

Flexor Carpi
Ulnaris

Brachialis

Flexor Digitorum
Profundus

Flexor Pollicis
Longus

Flexor Digitorum Superficialis

Anterior
Deltoid

Pectoralis
Major

Biceps
Brachii

Supraspinatus
Subscapularis
Pectoralis
Minor

Serratus
Anterior

Trapezius
Deltoid-
mid fibres

Deltoid-
posterior
fibres

Rhomboids
Supraspinatus
Infraspinatus
Teres Minor
Serratus
Anterior

Triceps
Brachii

GENERAL SAFETY INSTRUCTIONS
- Check all equipment before use.
- In all exercises where the lifter lies on the bench keep head, shoulders and hips in firm contact with the bench. Bend the knees and keep feet flat on the floor to maintain stability.
- If you do not have a bench at home lie on your back on the floor with knees bent, and feet flat on the floor hip width apart.

BREATHING
- Breathing should be rhythmical during each repetition.
- For All Pressing Exercises;
- Breathe IN on the effort.
- Breathe OUT as you return to start position.
- In all those exercises where the action expands the rib cage:
  - Breathe IN at the start, Breathe OUT on effort e.g. Straight Arm Pullover, Bent Arm Pullover, Dumb-bell Flys, Seated Chest Press.

CHEST AND SHOULDERS **CHARTEX**

DUMB-BELL EXERCISES

1 BENT ARM DUMB-BELL FLYS

Major Muscles Working:
Pectoralis Major, Anterior Fibres of Deltoid, Triceps Brachii,
(Biceps Brachii – as Elbows are flexed).

- Grasp dumb-bells with knuckles facing outwards.

- Bend arms as dumb-bells are lowered sideways under
  control, until they are slightly below the level of the shoulders.

- If lying on the floor lower the dumb-bells down until the elbows
  touch the floor level with the shoulders.

- Press up to bring dumb-bells back to start position.

START POSITION

2 DUMB-BELL BENCH PRESS

Major Muscles Working:
Pectoralis Major, Anterior Fibres of Deltoid, Triceps Brachii.

- Grasp dumb-bells with knuckles facing outwards.

- Lower dumb-bells under control until they are level with
  the chest.

- If lying on the floor lower dumb-bells down until the
  elbows touch the floor at the side of your body.

- Press up to start position.

**N.B. This exercise is particularly beneficial in the
development of power and muscular control in the
chest and front of shoulders.**

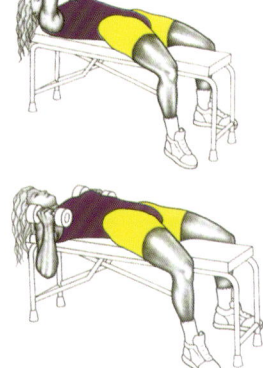

START POSITION

3 INCLINE DUMB-BELL PRESS

Major Muscles Working:
Pectoralis Major, Anterior Fibres of Deltoid, Triceps Brachii.

- Grasp dumb-bells with knuckles facing outwards and bring
  them up to shoulder level.

- Press the dumb-bells up until arms are straight.

- Lower under control to start position.

**N.B. If doing this exercise at home sit back in a chair
keeping hips and back in firm contact with the chair and
remain upright throughout the exercise.**

**N.B. This exercise concentrates resistance on the upper
fibres of the Pectoralis Major muscle in the chest, upper
arms and front of shoulders.**

START POSITION

DUMB-BELL EXERCISES

4 STRAIGHT ARM DUMB-BELL FLYS

START POSITION

Major Muscles Working:
Pectoralis Major, Anterior Fibres of Deltoid, Muscles involved in gripping.

- Grasp dumb-bells with knuckles facing outwards.

- Keeping arms straight lower dumb-bells under control, until level with the shoulders.

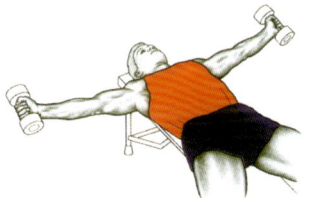

- If lying on the floor lower the dumb-bells down with arms straight until the arms touch the floor level with the shoulders.

- Bring the dumb-bells up to start position keeping the arms straight.

5 DECLINE DUMB-BELL PRESS

START POSITION

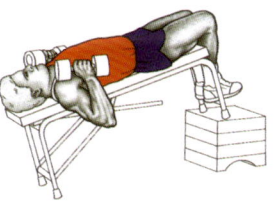

Major Muscles Working:
Pectoralis Major, Anterior Fibres of Deltoid, Triceps Brachii.

- Grasp dumb-bells with knuckles facing outwards and bring them to chest level.

- Press the dumb-bells up until arms are straight.

- Lower under control to start position.

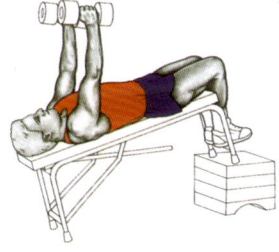

N.B. This exercise concentrates resistance on the lower fibres of Pectoralis Major, upper arms and front of shoulders.

CHARTEX

CHEST AND SHOULDERS

BARBELL EXERCISES

6 STRAIGHT ARM PULLOVER

Major Muscles Working:
Pectoralis Major, Anterior Fibres of Deltoid, Triceps, Muscles involved in gripping, Shoulder is stabilized by "Rotator Cuff" group.

- Grasp bar with hands shoulder width apart.

- Keeping arms straight gradually extend range of movement over the initial 3 or 4 repetitions to reach the finish position.

- Return under control to start position.

N.B. A Spotter must be used as shown.

START POSITION

7 BENT ARM PULLOVER

Major Muscles Working:
Pectoralis Major, Anterior Fibres of Deltoid, Biceps Brachii, Brachialis, Triceps, Latissimus Dorsi, Teres Major, "Rotator Cuff" group, Muscles involved in gripping.

- Grasp bar with hands shoulder width apart – bar resting on the chest.

- Keeping elbows bent lift bar over the face gradually extending range of movement over the initial 3 or 4 repetitions to bring the bar behind and below the head as shown.

- Return under control to start position.

N.B. A Spotter must be used as shown.

START POSITION

8 BARBELL CHEST PRESS

Major Muscles Working:
Pectoralis Major and Minor, Anterior Fibres of Deltoid, Triceps Brachii, Muscles involved in gripping.

- Grasp bar with the hands slightly wider than shoulder width.

- Press bar vertically above chest until arms are straight.

- Return under control to start position.

N.B. A Spotter must be used as shown.

START POSITION

SHOULDERS, UPPER ARM AND UPPER BACK MUSCLES

MAJOR MUSCLES WORKING

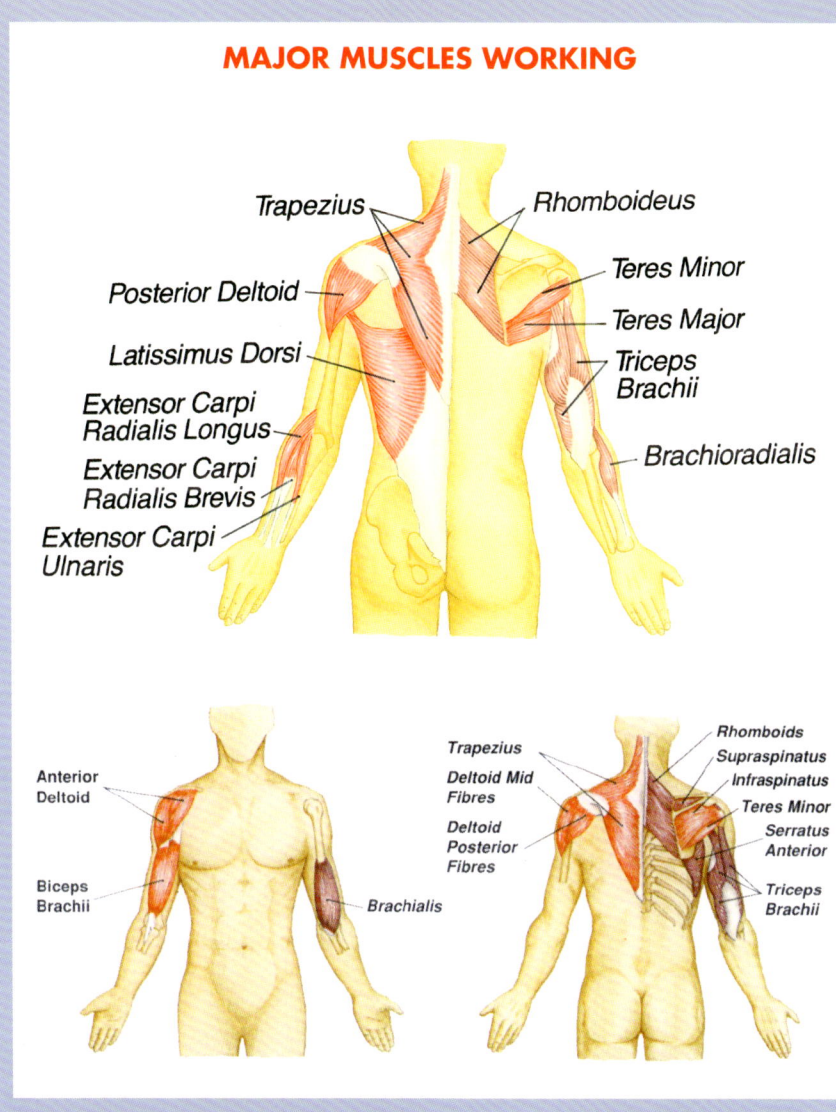

Trapezius

Rhomboideus

Posterior Deltoid

Teres Minor

Latissimus Dorsi

Teres Major

Triceps Brachii

Extensor Carpi Radialis Longus

Extensor Carpi Radialis Brevis

Brachioradialis

Extensor Carpi Ulnaris

Anterior Deltoid

Biceps Brachii

Brachialis

Trapezius

Deltoid Mid Fibres

Deltoid Posterior Fibres

Rhomboids

Supraspinatus

Infraspinatus

Teres Minor

Serratus Anterior

Triceps Brachii

GENERAL SAFETY INSTRUCTIONS

- Check all equipment before use.
- Place feet slightly wider than hip width apart to provide a firm and well balanced base.
- In standing exercises keep chest raised and body erect.

BREATHING

- Breathing should be rhythmical during each repetition.
- Breathe IN on the effort.
- Breathe OUT as you return to start position.

DUMB-BELL EXERCISES

DUMB-BELL "RAISES"

START POSITION

For maximum benefit in each of these "RAISE" exercises take dumb-bells to finish positions as illustrated.

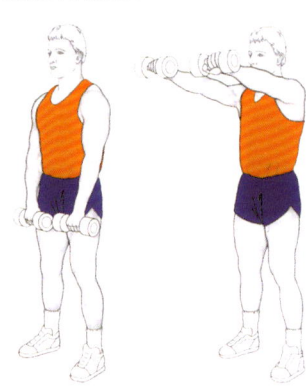

1 FORWARD RAISE

Major Muscles Working:
Anterior and Mid Fibres of Deltoid, Clavicular Fibres of Pectoralis Major and Triceps.

- Standing with feet shoulder width apart, knees slightly bent, grasp dumb-bells with overhand grip.

- Keeping arms straight, raise dumb-bells up directly in front of shoulders.

- Return under control to start position.

2 LATERAL RAISE

START POSITION

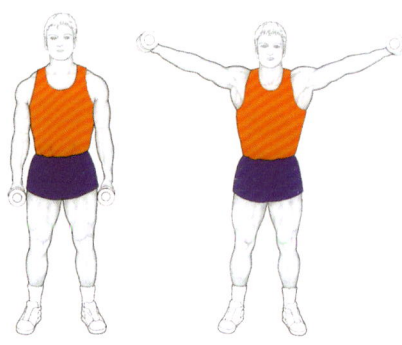

Major Muscles Working:
Mid and Anterior Fibres of Deltoid, Supraspinatus, Triceps, "Rotator Cuff" Muscle group.

- Standing with feet shoulder width apart, knees slightly bent, grasp dumb-bells, knuckles facing outwards.

- Keeping arms straight raise the dumb-bells up and away from side of body above shoulder level.

- Return under control to start position.

3 BENT FORWARD LATERAL RAISE

START POSITION

THIS IS AN ADVANCED EXERCISE

Major Muscles Working:
Posterior Fibres of Deltoid, Lower Trapezius, Rhomboids, Teres Major, Teres Minor, Infraspinatus and Triceps.

- Squat into start position, back straight, feet shoulder width apart.

- Grasp dumb-bells, knuckles facing outwards.

- Keeping arms straight raise dumb-bells up, away and back until just above shoulder level.

- Return under control to start position.

DUMB-BELL EXERCISES

4 DUMB-BELL PRESS

Major Muscles Working:
Deltoid, Serratus Anterior, Triceps Brachii,
Upper Fibres of Trapezius, Pectoralis Minor.

• Stand with feet shoulder width apart with knees slightly bent.

• Grasp dumb-bells firmly, knuckles facing outwards and press vertically from the shoulders until the arms are straight.

• This exercise is particularly beneficial in the development of power and muscular control in the shoulder area.

• Return under control to start position.

5 SINGLE ARM DUMB-BELL ROWING

START POSITION

Major Muscles Working:
Posterior Fibres of Deltoid, Rhomboids, Biceps Brachii, Brachialis, Infraspinatus, Teres Major and Teres Minor, Supraspinatus.

• Stand with feet slightly wider than hip width apart, knees slightly bent, back straight bending at the hips.

• Keep body in the start position throughout this exercise.

• Pull dumb-bell up to side of chest.

• Return under control to start position.

6 SHOULDER ABDUCTION THROUGH FLEXION

START POSITION

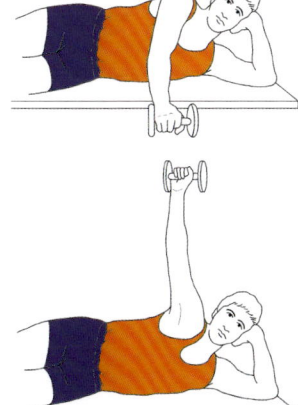

Major Muscles Working:
Posterior Deltoid, Latissimus Dorsi, Triceps, Teres Major.

• Lie on your side, knees slightly bent, head supported by the hand as shown.

• Grasp hold of dumb-bell and keeping arm straight raise the dumb-bell until the arm is directly above the shoulder.

• Return under control to start position.

BARBELL EXERCISES

7 STANDING SHOULDER PRESS

Major Muscles Working:
Deltoid, Serratus Anterior, Triceps Brachii, Upper Fibres of Trapezius, Muscles involved in gripping.

- Assume the "Get Set" position.
  (See Dead Lift exercise - page 37).

- Grasp bar firmly with hands shoulder width apart and bring it up to rest across the top of chest.

- Keep back straight throughout the exercise.

- Press the bar up until arms are straight.

- Return under control to start position.

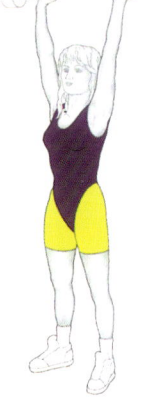

START POSITION

8 SEATED SHOULDER PRESS

Major Muscles Working:
Deltoid, Serratus Anterior, Triceps Brachii, Upper Fibres of Trapezius, Pectoralis Major, Muscles involved in gripping.

- Place feet more than shoulder width apart for stability.

- Keep back straight throughout the exercise as you press the bar up until arms are straight.

- Greater effort from the shoulders, arms and upper back muscles is required in this position.

- This exercise can also be performed with the bar behind the neck.

- Return under control to start position.

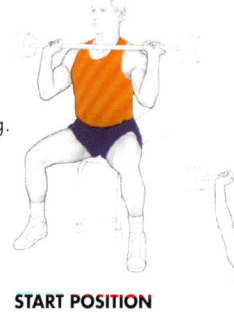

START POSITION

9 BENT FORWARD ROWING

Major Muscles Working:
Posterior Fibres of Deltoid, Biceps Brachii, Brachialis, Rhomboids, Teres Major, Teres Minor, Infraspinatus, Lower Trapezius.

- Standing with feet shoulder width apart adopt a semi-squat position with back straight.

- Keep body in the start position throughout the exercise.

- Grasp bar with the hands wider than shoulder width apart.

- Pull the bar up to touch the chest.

- Return under control to start position.

START POSITION

Exercise Variations:	Major Area Developed:
1 Pull bar to Shoulders	Upper Back
2 Pull bar to Mid Chest	Middle Back
3 Pull bar to Stomach	Lower Back

DUMB-BELL EXERCISES

10 PRESS BEHIND NECK

Major Muscles Working:
Deltoid, Serratus Anterior, Triceps Brachii,
Upper Fibres of Trapezius, Muscles involved in gripping.

- Assume the "Get Set" position.
  (See Dead Lift exercise - page 37).

- Grasp bar firmly with hands slightly wider than shoulder
  width apart and bring the bar up to rest across the back
  of the shoulders.

- Set head slightly forward to allow bar to be pressed
  vertically until arms are straight.

- Keep back straight throughout the exercise.

- Return under control to start position.

START POSITION

11 UPRIGHT ROWING

Major Muscles Working:
Deltoid, Serratus Anterior, Triceps Brachii,
Upper Fibres of Trapezius, Muscles involved in gripping.

- Assume the "Get Set" position.
  (See Dead Lift exercise - page 37).

- Grasp the bar with an overhand grip 6" apart
  and ensure feet are shoulder width apart.

- Keep back straight, elbows close to side.

- Gripping firmly raise bar up to chin with elbows held high.

- Return under control to start position fully extending the arms.

START POSITION

MAJOR MUSCLES WORKING

Gluteus Medius

Gluteus Minimus

Vastus Lateralis

Vastus Intermedius

Rectus Femoris

Gluteus Maximus

Vastus Medialis

Biceps Femoris

Semimembranosus

Semitendinosus

Tibialis Anterior

Lateral Head of Gastrocnemius

Medial Head of Gastrocnemius

Peroneus { Longus Brevis

Gastrocnemius

Soleus

Extensor Digitorum Longus

Extensor Hallucis Longus

Longissimus Dorsi

Spinalis Dorsi

Ilio Costalis Lumborum

GENERAL SAFETY INSTRUCTIONS

- Check all equipment before use.
- A Spotter must be used when doing Back Squats.
- Squat until top of thighs are parallel with ground.
- In all "Squat" exercises place feet slightly wider than hip width apart to provide a firm and well balanced base.

Keep the back straight

BREATHING

• For Squat Exercises -
Due to rapid progress when doing these exercises breathing is as follows: Breathe IN at start position, lower to Squat, then drive upwards. Breathe OUT as you return to start position.

•All Other Exercises -
Breathing should be rhythmical during each repetition.
Breathe IN on the effort. Breathe OUT as you return to start position.

DUMB-BELL EXERCISES

1 DUMB-BELL SQUATS

Major Muscles Working:
Quadriceps Muscle group, Gluteus Maximus,
Muscles of the Lower Back
(Strongly assisted by the Hamstrings).

• Grasp dumb-bells with knuckles facing outwards
  and rest them on the shoulders.

• Place feet shoulder width apart and squat down to a
  balanced position until you touch a chair with your bottom.

• Keep the back straight and chest raised as you squat.

• Thrust back up to start position.

START POSITION

2 DUMB-BELL FRONT SQUAT

Major Muscles Working:
Quadriceps (Rectus Femoris and Vasti Muscles),
Gluteus Maximus, Muscles of the Lower Back
(Strongly assisted by the Hamstrings).

• Grasp each end of the dumb-bell with both hands and rest
  it on the top of the chest.

• Place feet shoulder width apart and squat down to a
  balanced position until you touch a chair with your bottom.

• Keep the back straight and the dumb-bell held high on the
  top of the chest as you squat.

• Thrust back up to start position.

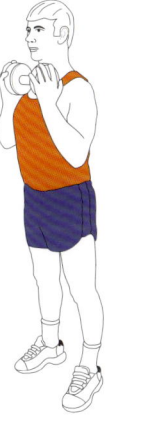

START POSITION

3 DUMB-BELL SPLIT SQUATS (Lunges)

Major Muscles Working:
Quadriceps, Gluteus Maximus, Tensor Fascia Latae, Muscles
of the Lower Back (Strongly assisted by the Hamstrings).

• Grasp dumb-bells with knuckles facing outwards and hold
  them by your side with arms straight.

• Keeping back straight lunge forward with the right foot and
  lower the body down until the thigh is at right angles with the
  calf.

• Thrust back to the start position then repeat with the left leg
  lunging forward.

START POSITION

CHARTEX

LEG MUSCLES

LEG MUSCLES CHARTEX

4 STANDING CALF RAISE

Major Muscles Working:
Gastrocnemius and Soleus.

- Standing, place the balls of your feet on the edge of a bench or step as shown.

- Grasp hold of dumb-bells with knuckles facing outwards and rest them on the shoulders.

- Keeping the back and legs straight throughout the exercise, lower the heels down then push up on to the toes to achieve full range of movement at the ankle.

START POSITION

5 SEATED CALF RAISE

Major Muscles Working:
Gastrocnemius and Soleus.

- Sitting, place the balls of your feet on the edge of a low bench or step as shown.

- Grasp dumb-bells with knuckles facing upwards and rest them as close to the knees as possible – put padding on the knees for comfort if required.

- Keeping back straight lower the heels down then push up on to the toes to achieve full range of movement at the ankle.

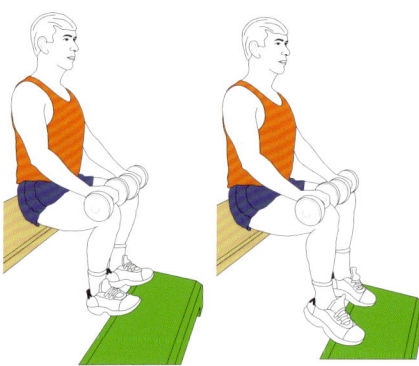

START POSITION

6 STEP-UPS

Major Muscles Working:
Quadriceps, Hamstrings, Gastrocnemius, Soleus and Lower Back Muscles.

- Stand on a low bench or step as shown.

- Grasping the dumb-bells with knuckles facing outwards rest them on the shoulders.

- Keeping a steady rhythm step up and down alternately. Lead first with the right leg, then change to leading with left leg after 10 step ups.

- Ensure you place the whole foot firmly on the bench and floor at each step.

- To increase workload step up on a higher bench.

START POSITION

BARBELL EXERCISES

7 BACK SQUATS

Major Muscles Working:
Quadriceps Muscle group, Gluteus Maximus,
Muscles of the Lower Back (Strongly assisted by the Hamstrings).

- Assume the "Get Set" position. (See Dead Lift exercise - page 37).

- Grasp the barbell and bring it up to rest on the back of the shoulders.

- Keep back straight and chest raised.

- Squat down until the thigh is at right angles with the calf.

- Thrust back up to start position.

START POSITION

8 FRONT SQUATS

Major Muscles Working:
Quadriceps Muscle group, Gluteus Maximus, Muscles
of the Lower Back (Strongly assisted by the Hamstrings).

- Assume the "Get Set" position. (See Dead Lift exercise - page 37).

- Grasp the barbell and bring it up to rest across the front
  of the shoulders.

- Keep elbows high, chest raised and feet shoulder width apart.

- Keep back straight.

- Squat down until thigh is at right angles with the calf.

- Thrust back up to start position.

START POSITION

9 BARBELL SPLIT SQUATS (Lunges)

Major Muscles Working:
Quadriceps Muscle group, Gluteus Maximus,
Muscles of the Lower Back
(Strongly assisted by the Hamstrings).

- Assume the "Get Set" position.
  (See Dead Lift exercise - page 37).

- Grasp the barbell and bring it up to rest
  on the front of the shoulders.

- Step forward into split position. Lower the
  body down and forwards towards front foot,
  keeping back straight.

- Thrust back up to start position.

START POSITION

CHARTEX

LEG MUSCLES

LEG MUSCLES CHARTEX

10 STANDING CALF RAISE

Major Muscles Working:
Gastrocnemius and Soleus.

- Assume the "Get Set" position.
  (See Dead Lift exercise - page 37).

- Grasp the barbell and bring it up to rest across
  the back of the shoulders and keep back straight
  throughout the exercise.

- Standing, place the balls of your feet on the edge
  of a low bench or step as shown.

- Lower heels as shown to permit full range of
  movement at the ankle joint.

- Keep legs straight as you drive up on to the toes.

START POSITION

11 SEATED CALF RAISE

Major Muscles Working:
Gastrocnemius and Soleus.

- Sitting, place the balls of your feet on the edge
  of a low bench or step as shown.

- Place bar as close to knees as possible
  – padding can be used for comfort if required.

- Lower heels as shown to permit full range
  of movement at the ankle.

- Push up on to the toes.

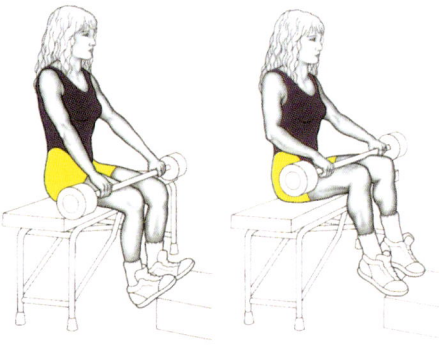

START POSITION

12 STEP-UPS

Major Muscles Working:
Quadriceps, Hamstrings, Gastrocnemius,
Soleus, also Lower Back and Abdominal
Muscles to keep Spine in good alignment.

- Assume the "Get Set" position to bring the
  bar up to the start position.
  (See Dead Lift page 37).

- This is a rhythmic sequence of stepping up
  and down alternately.

- Place the whole foot firmly on the bench
  and floor at each step.

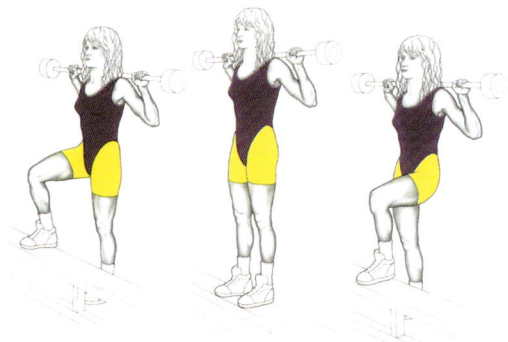

START POSITION

LEG, TRUNK, SHOULDER AND ARM MUSCLES

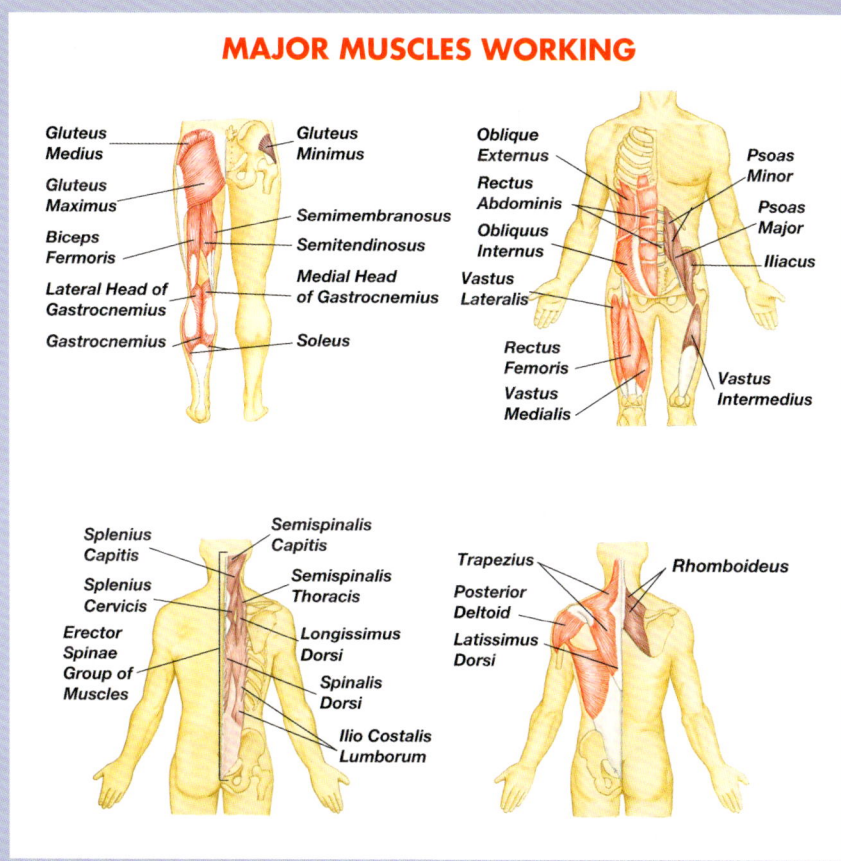

MAJOR MUSCLES WORKING

Gluteus Medius
Gluteus Maximus
Biceps Femoris
Lateral Head of Gastrocnemius
Gastrocnemius

Gluteus Minimus
Semimembranosus
Semitendinosus
Medial Head of Gastrocnemius
Soleus

Oblique Externus
Rectus Abdominis
Obliquus Internus
Vastus Lateralis
Rectus Femoris
Vastus Medialis

Psoas Minor
Psoas Major
Iliacus
Vastus Intermedius

Splenius Capitis
Splenius Cervicis
Erector Spinae Group of Muscles

Semispinalis Capitis
Semispinalis Thoracis
Longissimus Dorsi
Spinalis Dorsi
Ilio Costalis Lumborum

Trapezius
Posterior Deltoid
Latissimus Dorsi

Rhomboideus

GENERAL SAFETY INSTRUCTIONS

- Check all equipment before use.
- In all lifting movements from the floor maintain a straight back.
- Warm up with light weights.

BREATHING

- Breathing should be rhythmical during each repetition.
- For all Barbell and Dumb-bell exercises:
  Breathe IN as the Bar/Dumb-bell is lifted. Breathe OUT as you return to start position.

DUMB-BELL EXERCISES

1 SINGLE ARM ROWING-TRUNK ROTATION

Major Muscles Working:
Latissimus Dorsi, Trunk Rotators, Shoulder Muscles.

- Place feet hip width apart, knees slightly bent, back straight and head up.

- The dumb-bell is held low and across the body.

- Pull dumb-bell up high with trunk rotation.

- Breathe in as you lift and rotate, and out as you return to start position.

START POSITION

2 LATERAL FLEXION

Major Muscles Working:
Internal and External Obliques, Abdominal Muscles, Spinalis Dorsi, Longissimus Dorsi, Ilio Costalis Lumborum.

- Place feet wider than hip width apart and set hips slightly forward.

- Keeping legs and arm straight bend sideways against the resistance, breathing in.

- Breathe out as you return to start position before bending to the other side.

START POSITION

3 BENT FORWARD ROWING

Major Muscles Working:
Upper Fibres of Latissimus Dorsi, Posterior Fibres of Deltoid, Rhomboids, Lower Fibres of Trapezius.

- Place feet hip width apart, keep back straight, knees slightly bent.

- Breathing in, pull the dumb-bells up to the side of the trunk with elbows high.

- Breathe out as you return under control to the start position.

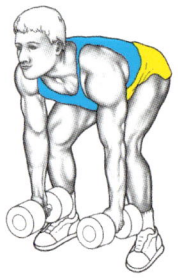

START POSITION

BARBELL EXERCISES

4 DEAD LIFT

Major Muscles Working:
Gluteus Maximus, Quadriceps, Hamstrings
and Erector Spinae group of Muscles.

- Assume the "Get Set" position.

- Grasp barbell with hands shoulder
  width apart.

- Adopt a squat position with head up,
  hips down, back straight, feet hip width apart.

- Keeping the back straight drive strongly with the
  legs to assume the upright position.

- Keep barbell close to the body throughout the movement.

- Return under control to "Get Set" position.

GET SET POSITION

START POSITION

5 SHOULDER SHRUG

Major Muscles Working:
Trapezius.

- Assume the "Get Set" position to bring
  the bar to the start position.
  (See Dead Lift above).

- Stand erect with bar resting across the thighs.

- Breathing in, pull the shoulders up towards the ears.

- Breathe out as you return under control to start position.

START POSITION

6 HIGH PULL-UP

Major Muscles Working:
Quadriceps, Hamstrings, Trapezius, Deltoid,
Erector Spinae group of Muscles.

- With a wider than shoulder width grip assume the
  "Get Set" position. (See Dead Lift above).

- In one movement drive high up on to the toes
  pulling bar vigorously to the top of the chest.

- Return under control to start position.

START POSITION

CHAPTER X

LEGS, TRUNK, SHOULDER AND ARM

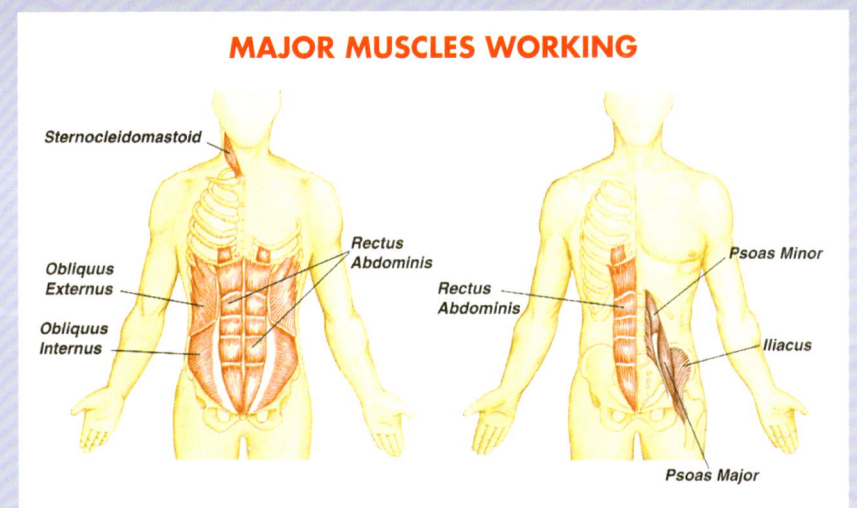

MAJOR MUSCLES WORKING

(Labels: Sternocleidomastoid, Obliquus Externus, Obliquus Internus, Rectus Abdominis, Rectus Abdominis, Psoas Minor, Iliacus, Psoas Major)

GENERAL SAFETY INSTRUCTIONS

- Keep LOWER BACK and PELVIS in contact with the floor during all abdominal exercises.
- Use the hands to SUPPORT THE HEAD during any of the exercises, if required. This will relieve pressure on the neck muscles.
- Maintain a rhythmical action controlling the upward and downward movement.
- Aim for a minimum of 10 repetitions at each chosen exercise. To progress, gradually increase repetitions.

N.B. If suffering from back problems consult your Doctor, Physiotherapist or Specialist before doing these exercises.

BREATHING

- Maintain a controlled rhythmical breathing action during each sit-up.
- Breathe OUT to the count of ONE as you raise up.
- Breathe IN to the count of 2/3 as you lower down to start position.

ABDOMINAL EXERCISES

1 HANDS TO KNEES SIT-UP Beginner Level

To strengthen: Rectus Abdominis.

- For complete beginner start with pillow under head and shoulders.

- Keep arms straight & feet flat on floor.

- Raise head & shoulders off the ground stretching hands to touch knees, looking straight ahead.

START POSITION

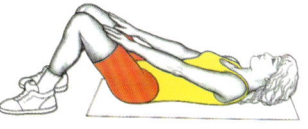
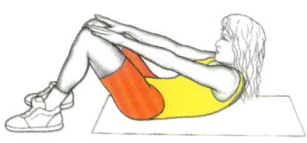

2 OBLIQUE SIT-UP HANDS TO KNEES Beginner Level

To strengthen:
Internal/External Obliques and Rectus Abdominis.

- For complete beginner start with pillow under head and shoulders.

- Keep arms straight and feet flat on the floor.

- Raise head & shoulders off the ground stretching hands to touch left knee, looking over to the left.

- Repeat 10 times to each knee.

START POSITION

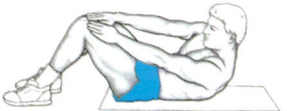

3 SHOULDER RAISE SIT-UP Intermediate Level

To strengthen: Rectus Abdominis.

- Keep feet flat on floor.

- Place hands behind head **for support only**.

- Raise head and shoulders off the ground looking slightly up.

START POSITION

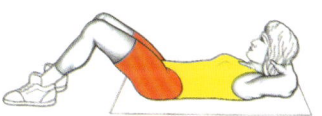
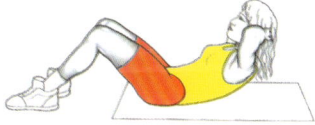

4 CRUNCH ABDOMINALS - FEET CROSSED
Intermediate Level

To strengthen: Rectus Abdominis.

- Keep thighs at right angles to the hip.

- Keeping hands on side of head bring elbows up to touch thighs.

- ALTERNATIVE EXERCISE – Right elbow to left knee and vice versa.

N.B. This will exercise the Internal and External Obliques.

START POSITION

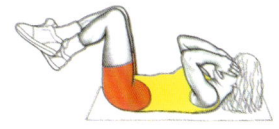

CHARTEX

ABDOMINAL EXERCISES

ABDOMINAL EXERCISES

5 OBLIQUE CRUNCH SIT-UP Intermediate Level

To strengthen:
Internal/External Obliques and Rectus Abdominis.

- Keep thigh at rights angles to the hip.

- Bring right elbow up and over to touch left knee.

- Repeat 10 times to each knee.

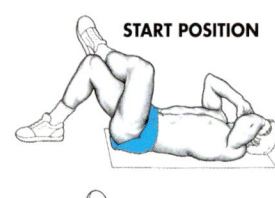

START POSITION

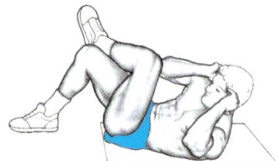

6 ALTERNATE ELBOW TO KNEE Intermediate Level

To strengthen:
Internal/External Obliques and Rectus Abdominis.

- Start Position is as for "Oblique Crunch Sit-up".

- Maintain controlled rhythmical action.

- Keep thighs at right angles to the hip when bringing elbow up and over to touch opposite knee.

- Keep hands on side of head.

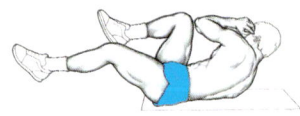

EXERCISE POSITION

7 SIT-UP - ARMS ACROSS CHEST Advanced Level

To strengthen:
Rectus Abdominis.

- Keep feet flat on the floor.

- Keep hands touching front of shoulders.

- Look straight ahead when you sit-up.

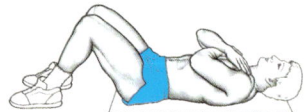

START POSITION

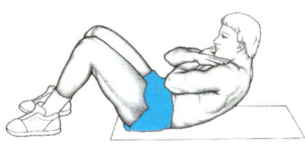

8 OBLIQUE SIT-UP - ARMS ACROSS CHEST
Advanced Level

To strengthen:
Internal/External Obliques and Rectus Abdominis.

- Keep feet flat on the floor.

- Keeping hands on front of shoulders, bring right elbow up and over towards left knee.

- Repeat 10 times to each knee.

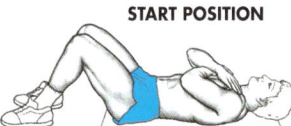

START POSITION

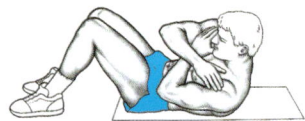

BACK EXERCISES

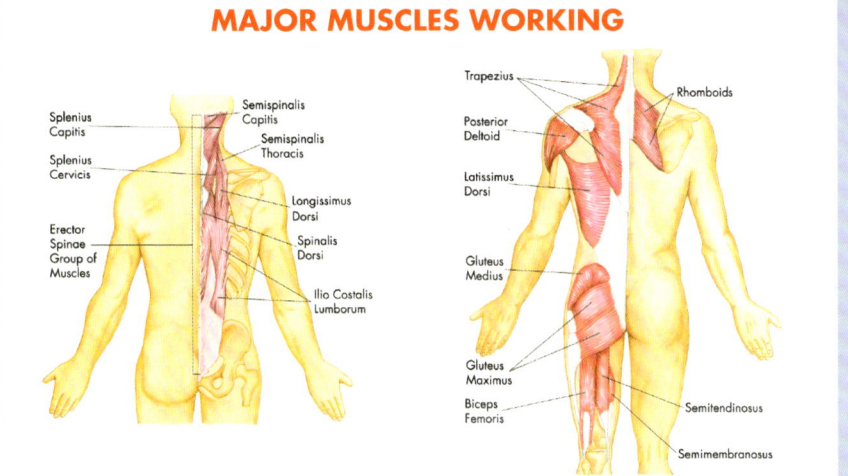

MAJOR MUSCLES WORKING

Splenius Capitis
Splenius Cervicis
Erector Spinae Group of Muscles
Semispinalis Capitis
Semispinalis Thoracis
Longissimus Dorsi
Spinalis Dorsi
Ilio Costalis Lumborum

Trapezius
Posterior Deltoid
Latissimus Dorsi
Gluteus Medius
Gluteus Maximus
Biceps Femoris
Rhomboids
Semitendinosus
Semimembranosus

GENERAL SAFETY INSTRUCTIONS

- Place one or two pillows under hips and abdominals for support. Maintain the body in a comfortable extended position in order to avoid hyper-extension of the lower back.

- Hold all extended positions in the strengthening exercises for a minimum count of three.

- Return slowly and under control to start position – relax the muscles – then repeat the exercise.

- Aim for a minimum of **five repetitions** at chosen exercise.

- To progress increase repetitions gradually and hold extended positions longer.

N.B. If suffering from back problems consult your Doctor, Physiotherapist or Specialist before doing these exercises.

BREATHING

- Maintain a controlled rhythmical breathing action during each repetition.

- Breathe **IN** and **OUT** as you hold the extended position.

BACK EXERCISES **CHARTEX**

BACK EXERCISES

1 SHOULDER RAISE

START POSITION

To strengthen:
Erector Spinae group of Muscles.

• Keep head and neck in neutral alignment when raising shoulders and head off the ground.

• Keep feet in firm contact with the ground as shown.

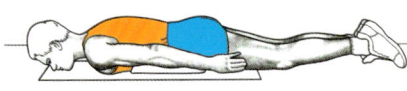
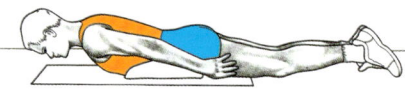

2 DOUBLE LEG RAISE

START POSITION

To strengthen:
Gluteus Maximus, Spinalis Dorsi,
Ilio Costalis Lumborum.

• Rest forehead on hands and keep feet together, legs straight and toes pointed.

• Raise lower legs approximately 6 inches off the ground as shown.

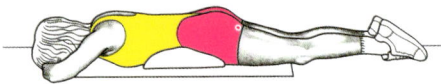
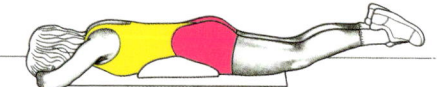

3 SHOULDER RAISE-HANDS
ON FOREHEAD

START POSITION

To strengthen:
Erector Spinae group of Muscles.

• Place back of hands on forehead, then raise head, arms and shoulders off the ground keeping head and neck in neutral alignment.

• Keep feet in firm contact with the ground as shown.

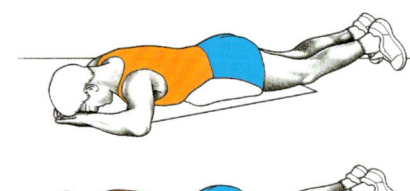
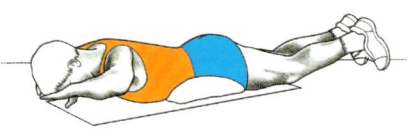

4 HIP FLEXION AND EXTENSION

START POSITION

To Work:
Psoas Major and Iliacus (At the front of the Hip),
Gluteus Maximus, Hamstrings.

• Keep back as straight as possible when flexing and extending the hip as shown.

5 LOWER BACK EXTENSION

START POSITION

To stretch the abdominals.

To stretch the anterior structures of the spine and puts lumbar spine into extended position.

• Raise head, shoulders and chest off the ground.

• Press hips and lower abdominals into the ground.

• Hold for a count of 10 to 15. Relax between repetitions.

6 SHOULDER AND LEG RAISE

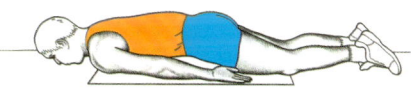

START POSITION

To strengthen:
Erector Spinae group, Gluteus Maximus.

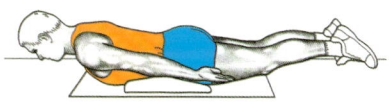

• Keep head and neck in neutral alignment when raising shoulders and head off the ground.

• Keep feet together, legs straight and toes pointed as you raise lower legs about 6 inches off the ground.

7 OPPOSITE ARM AND LEG RAISE

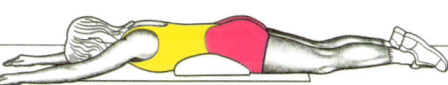

START POSITION

To strengthen:
Erector Spinae group, Gluteus Maximus.

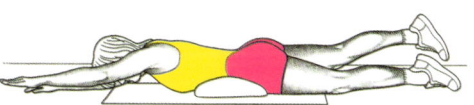

• Raise the left arm and right leg about 6 inches off the ground.

• As the left shoulder is raised off the ground keep head and neck in neutral alignment.

• Return to start and repeat, raising right arm and left leg.

8 SHOULDER AND LEG RAISE WITH HANDS ON FOREHEAD

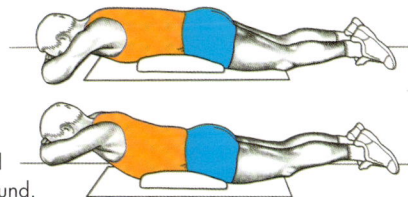

START POSITION

To strengthen:
Erector Spinae group, Gluteus Maximus.

• Rest forehead on hands, keep head and neck in neutral alignment when raising shoulders and head off the ground.

• Keep feet together, legs straight and toes pointed as you raise feet and lower legs about 6 inches off the ground.

9 STRAIGHT ARM AND LEG RAISE

START POSITION

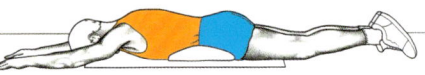

To strengthen:
Erector Spinae group, Gluteus Maximus.

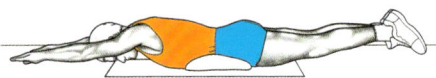

• With arms stretched out in front raise head, shoulders, arms and legs about 6 inches off the ground, keeping head and neck in neutral alignment.

• Keep toes pointed and legs straight.

10 LOWER BACK FLEXION

To stretch the lower back muscles.

To stretch posterior structures of spinal column and puts lower spine into flexed position.

Position 1

• Grasp hold of back of thighs.

Position 2

• Bring knees into the chest.

Position 3

• Take head up towards the knees.

• Hold either position 2 or 3 for the count of 3. Relax between each repetition.

11 BALANCED DORSAL RAISE ON INFLATABLE BALL

To strengthen:
Gluteals, Long Extensors of Lower Back and Hamstrings.

START POSITION

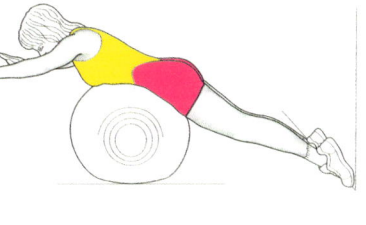

- Kneel down, balls of feet against the wall, hands on the ball in front of you.

- Lower your upper body and hips onto the ball and roll forwards by straightening your knees to achieve a good neutral spinal alignment with a long neck and balanced head position.

- Take your arms off the ball and lift them forward to a superman position.

EXERCISE MOVEMENT

- Lift your upper body by tightening your gluteals (Buttocks) and extending the lower back.

- Keep your arms up and stretched forwards.

- Repeat the exercise.

- Return to start position by holding the ball and rolling back on your knees.

N.B. Upper Fibres of Trapezius, Rhomboids, Deltoid (Posterior Fibres), Pectoralis Major (Clavicular Fibres), and Hamstrings, work to hold the limbs in the extended position.

DON'T FORGET TO COOL DOWN AFTER TRAINING

COOL-DOWN EXERCISE ADVICE

Why you should Cool-Down after exercise/training

- It enables the body to adjust from exercise to rest, lowering the heart rate in a controlled way.
- It helps the body deal with removal of waste products from the muscles during the recovery process and reduce muscle soreness.
- It facilitates muscular relaxation and by stretching helps to prevent muscle shortening.

How to Cool-Down

- Cool Down by gradually decreasing the intensity of cardio-respiratory exercise over 6 to 8 minutes. (See - page 10).
- Follow this aerobic exercise with stretching exercises that were done in the warm-up.
- Hold each stretch for about 10 - 15 seconds and do a minimum of 2 repetitions at each stretch.

Soleus Stretch
(Calf Muscle)

Gastrocnemius Stretch
(Calf Muscle)

Hamstring Stretch
(Back of Thighs)

Quads Stretch
(Front of Thighs)

Adductor Stretch
(Inside of Thighs)

Lumbar Spine and Gluteals Stretch
(Lower Back and Hips)

COOL-DOWN EXERCISES

CHARTEX

COOL-DOWN EXERCISE ADVICE

Lower Back Stretch

Cat Stretch
(Spine)

Lateral Flexion of Spine

Anterior Shoulder/Chest Stretch
(Front of Shoulder)

Posterior Shoulder Stretch
(Back of Shoulder)

Triceps Stretch
(Back of Upper Arm)

Introduction

Any exercise or training can be both physically and mentally draining and any active person can benefit from improving their nutritional intake and dietary habits. This means eating a healthy, varied and balanced diet each day, which supplies enough carbohydrate, is low in fat, contains good quality protein and is balanced in all other nutrients. Careful timing of meals and snacks around training schedules is also equally important.

Energy for exercise and training

Individual differences such as age, gender, height and weight, muscle mass and activity levels mean that energy requirements vary from person to person and from day to day. Typically men and women who engage in regular exercise have higher energy needs than less active people, whilst men require more energy than women because of their larger muscle mass.

Carbohydrates, fats and protein all provide the body with energy, although protein is of less importance as an energy source for exercise. The preferred fuel source for exercise is glucose, formed from the breakdown of carbohydrates. In order to eat sufficient carbohydrate to fuel activity, the amount of fat must be kept to a minimum to avoid unwanted weight gain, which is consistent with healthy eating guidelines.

Carbohydrate, as glucose, is the most important energy source for exercise because it is the only fuel that can power intense exercise for prolonged periods. Glucose is stored as glycogen in the muscles and liver where it is readily available as a source of energy for the body. However our muscles are only capable of storing a limited amount of glycogen and during exercise this is used to supply muscles with energy to contract. As glycogen is burned up, and as stores decrease, both physical and mental fatigue sets in. The amount of each energy source used during exercise depends on the type of exercise, its intensity and duration, the frequency of sessions, individual fitness levels and dietary intakes. To try and delay fatigue in any exercise lasting around an hour or more, it is important to start with optimal stores of glycogen. This is achieved by eating plenty of carbohydrate rich foods which can be either sugary or starchy. However, it is healthier to eat more starchy carbohydrates as they are also valuable sources of other nutrients.

Eating before training

Eating a varied and well balanced diet should ensure that stores of glycogen in the muscles and liver are adequate to supply enough energy to perform well and delay fatigue. It is ideal to eat a carbohydrate rich meal or snack with a drink between 2 - 3 hours before any strenuous training to 'top up' the glycogen stores. Avoiding fatty foods is important as they take longest to leave the stomach and may cause discomfort. For some people who are unable to eat before intense exercise it can be helpful to avoid solid food and replace with low fat milk, yoghurt or yoghurt shake or smoothie.

During training

It may be necessary for some highly active individuals to take sports drinks and solid snacks e.g. cereal bars, bananas and raisins with them. It is advisable to plan ahead and decide when it is ideal to take a drink or snack break.

Food for recovery – eating immediately after training

To promote a rapid recovery in preparation for the next training session, it is useful to replace the energy and fluid that you have used as quickly as possible. If your sessions are intense and you are training hard once or twice a day, the best time to do this is soon after exercise when muscles are most efficient at storing glycogen.

In this recovery phase, it is moderate to high glycaemic index carbohydrate rich foods which are absorbed quickly by the body and as such are good choices for refuelling muscles immediately after exercise. It is, however, very important to sit down to a high carbohydrate, balanced meal to provide other nutrients, as soon as possible.

Glycaemic index of some carbohydrate-rich foods

GI classification	Foods
Lower GI foods	Pulses, peas, beans and legumes Oat based cereal and oat products Pasta Raw fruit (not over-ripe) Milk and plain yoghurt
Intermediate or moderate GI foods	New potatoes Pitta bread, cereal bars Banana Dried fruit Honey
Higher GI foods	Bread (white and wholemeal) Corn or wheat based cereals Old potatoes and mashed potatoes Fruit juices Sweets Sports drinks

Fluid and Hydration

During exercise and training, loss of fluid through sweating can easily lead to dehydration and is a major cause of fatigue and poor performance and will reduce overall enjoyment of the activity. Not only does dehydration impair performance, it can also be dangerous causing heatstroke and increases the risk of injury. Keeping well hydrated is therefore essential to maintain both physical performance and concentration in any activity.

Practical tips for keeping hydrated

1 Drink plenty every day, throughout the day and especially before, during and after any activity.

2 A diet with plenty of fruit and vegetables also contributes to your fluid intake.

3 Make sure that you are well hydrated before any activity. Pale and plentiful urine is a good indication that you are drinking enough.

4 Carry a water bottle or two and keep refilling it with your chosen drink, sipping frequently during activity.

5 Waiting until you are thirsty is too late to start drinking, as you will already be dehydrated.

6 After any exercise or training session, it is important to replace your losses so remember to continue to drink to replace fluid losses.

7 Throughout the day, fruit juices, squashes, water, herbal and fruit teas are all good choices of fluid.

8 There are many commercial sports drinks widely available. Both hypotonic and isotonic sports drinks are convenient in promoting rapid rehydration in preparation for, during and in recovery from exercise and training. Isotonic drinks also supply carbohydrate as an additional energy source. Use sports drinks wisely and appropriately as overuse can cause dental erosion.

Nutrition for increasing muscle mass and strength

Despite the obsession with protein and muscle growth, additional energy is the key to an increase in muscle mass and ultimately strength. Although protein is laid down to form the cells which support the new tissue, the additional requirement is actually only a small amount each day. Inadequate amounts of carbohydrate to fuel training and inadequate energy intake will both impair the rate of increase in lean body mass. Additional amounts of some micronutrients are needed in the manufacture of the new tissue but the additional dietary energy required to promote the gain of lean body mass should also provide sufficient amounts of micronutrients.

• Follow a progressive resistance training programme that stimulates muscle development and growth.

• Eat 2 - 3 hours before and soon after resistance training sessions. Include a source of good quality protein in these meals or snacks e.g. milk with cereal, ham, egg, chicken or fish in a sandwich or jacket potato, prawns with noodles.

NUTRITIONAL ADVICE FOR TRAINING

• Aim to increase food intake by an additional 500 kcal/d. This additional food should be nutritious supplying carbohydrate to fuel the training sessions and adequate protein and micronutrients for the development and support of new tissue

• Include snacks as well as meals - nutritious high carbohydrate snacks which include a small amount of protein e.g. milkshake or tuna or peanut butter sandwiches are ideal between meals and particularly after training sessions

• Nutritious fluids such as milk, milk shakes, yoghurt shakes and fruit smoothies provide a source of energy, protein and other nutrients and can be easily consumed with meals or before and after training sessions.

A slightly higher protein intake can be useful for preserving muscle mass in active individuals on a low energy or energy restricted diet e.g. for low energy sportspeople such as gymnasts, dancers and endurance runners

Protein supplements are currently viewed as a popular and convenient way of increasing protein intake however they are rarely actually needed to increase protein intake as our British diet tends to supply more than enough protein to support the increased needs of any recreational sportsperson and competing athlete. Supplements are often expensive and do not compensate for a poor or inadequate dietary intake – it is much more effective to eat a good quality, well balanced diet and often far cheaper. Supplements are most useful for the travelling athlete or competitor who is unsure of the availability, hygiene and safety of food in other countries. However, be warned, if you compete and are eligible for drug testing many supplements are contaminated with traces of banned substances which can lead to positive doping tests!

CHOOSE WELL - EAT WELL - TRAIN WELL

WEIGHT TRAINING RECORD CARD

Example of a Weight Training Record Card

DATE	EXERCISE	RESISTANCE	REPETITIONS	SETS
	Dumb Bell Lateral Raise	5kg each Dumb Bell	10	2
	Dumb Bell Split Squats	8kg each Dumb Bell	10 to each leg	2

WEIGHT TRAINING RECORD CARD

Example of a Weight Training Record Card				
DATE	EXERCISE	RESISTANCE	REPETITIONS	SETS

Photocopy and record strength and fitness progress

WEIGHT TRAINING RECORD CARD

CHARTEX

There is a long history of investigation in mathematics with evidence that the Ancient Egyptians explored numbers and found patterns and connections in their work. From the time of ancient civilizations mathematics has been used to make sense of the world, and the universe in which we live.

This resource presents ten challenging mathematical investigations for pupils aged 8-11 along with guidance and suggested teaching approaches for teachers. As pupils work through the investigations they will need to use and apply skills and knowledge about number to 'do' mathematics. They will start to understand the importance of working systematically as they search for patterns and will need to think logically as they reason about what they discover. They will also need to make conjectures and test these as they work towards making generalizations.

To support non-specialist teachers we have suggested questions to ask pupils and also highlighted points that pupils might raise during the investigations.

Numicon and Investigations

Structured apparatus, such as Numicon Shapes and Number Rods, provide a visual, structured representation of number ideas. Using structured apparatus offers pupils a different way of exploring the ten investigations in this pack by enabling them to see relationships and connections between numbers.

This multi-sensory approach helps to demonstrate the important fact that numbers do not occur randomly, but form a highly organized system, containing many kinds of patterns. Inevitably, this approach will suggest different possibilities from those that emerge when children work with only with numerals.

In our experience, most pupils are confident, and motivated to embark on these investigations, and it is anticipated that the activities will be introduced to the whole class and returned to several times for collective review. These activities provide the opportunity for many of the investigations to be taken to levels that will challenge and interest even the most gifted and talented children.

Links with the National Curriculum

The National Curriculum encourages mathematics investigation, emphasizing the idea that mathematics should go beyond calculation and facts, and should be used to explore problems, model situations and share ideas. Each of the National Curriculum Programmes of Study, i.e. Ma2, Ma3 and Ma4, begins with a section on Using and Applying, which describes how mathematics should be used for problem solving, communication and reasoning. This is underlined in the 2009 Review of the National Curriculum. This set of activities includes Links to the National Curriculum 1999 Programme of Study for reference.

How to use this book

The ten investigations are ordered by level of challenge, although it is impossible to predict which aspects individual children will find the most difficult. Thus, we suggest various pathways and include some explanatory notes and suggestions about where the investigations might lead. In order that pupils get the most out of these investigations, we would recommend that teachers work through them before taking them into the classroom; first-hand experience of how an investigation may develop can be used to encourage meaningful questioning and dialogue in the classroom.

The investigations are structured as follows:

Introduction
A brief outline of the investigation with links to the National Curriculum programmes of study.

You Will Need...
A list of the resources required to do the activity.

Starting Point
A detailed outline of how to present the early part of the investigation, which is intended to be accessible to pupils at all levels.

The Main Part
Guidance and questions on how to develop the investigation. Lower achieving pupils may conclude at this stage.

What next?
How to continue and extend the work for the most able pupils, and some discussion pointers.

The essence of investigations is that they are open-ended and the 'What next?' section is intended to demonstrate this. It is vital to remember that the point chosen to finish an investigation, perhaps for a particular group of children, will be driven by several factors:

- Motivation – are the children enjoying the task, contributing to the discussion and producing results?

- Have the children reached a point when to go further would be taking them beyond the extent of their current knowledge and understanding?

- Time – no investigation should be continued at the expense of other areas of the curriculum.

In drawing investigations to a close, the emphasis should be on stopping the class activity, but leaving open the opportunity for the most motivated pupils to continue their explorations when time permits.

Finally, we would emphasize the importance of regarding investigative mathematical thinking as integral to pupils' mathematical experience. These investigations have been developed specifically to provide opportunities for pupils to explore number, and to reason and work systematically. However, the ways that are introduced to pupils for thinking about mathematical activities should reflect the key elements of 'doing mathematics' identified in the National Curriculum.

5

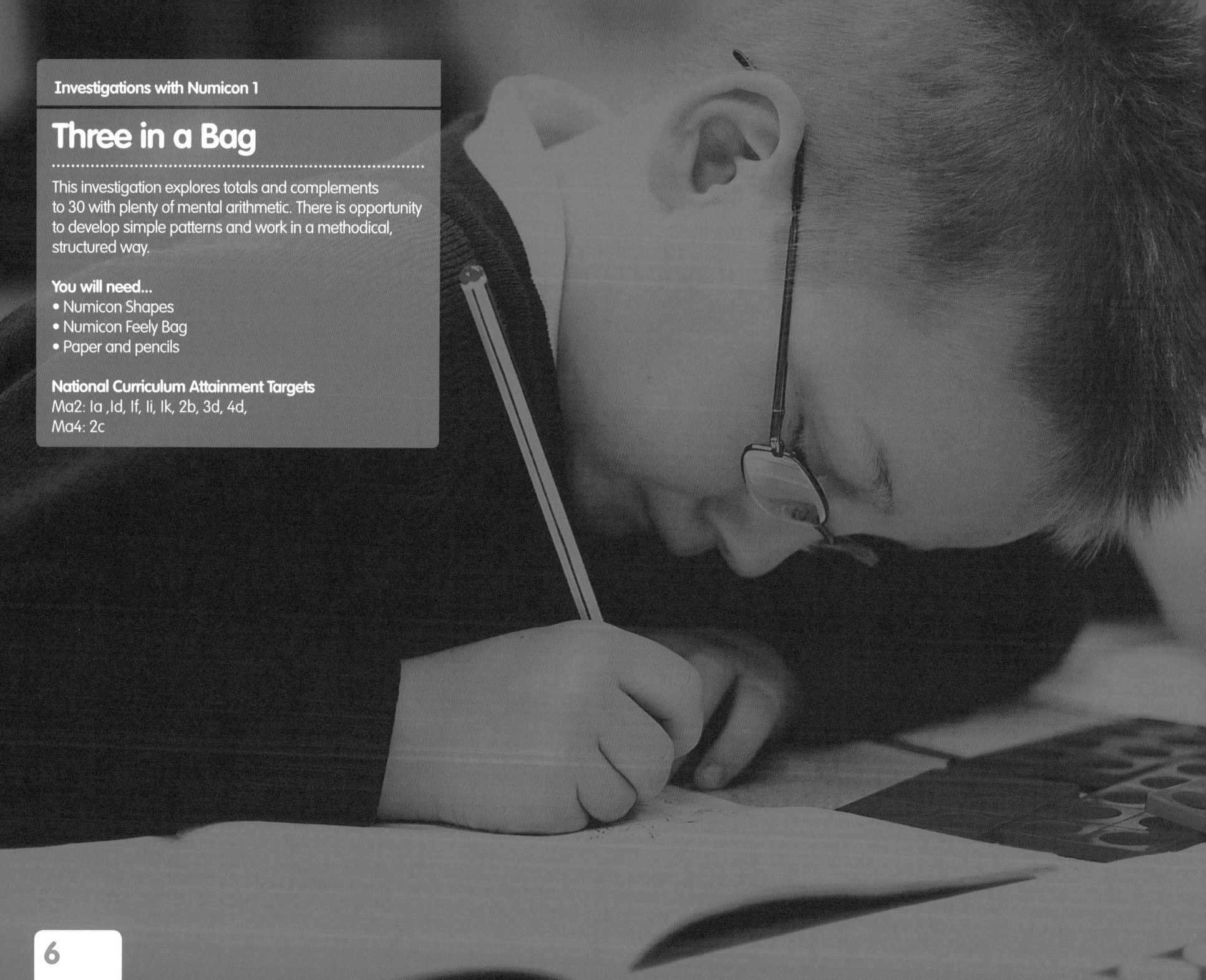

Three in a Bag

This investigation explores totals and complements to 30 with plenty of mental arithmetic. There is opportunity to develop simple patterns and work in a methodical, structured way.

You will need...
• Numicon Shapes
• Numicon Feely Bag
• Paper and pencils

National Curriculum Attainment Targets
Ma2: Ia ,Id, If, Ii, Ik, 2b, 3d, 4d,
Ma4: 2c

Starting Point

Pupils individually or with a partner should have access to a supply of Numicon Shapes.

1. Use the Feely Bag and put in three Numicon Shapes that total 15 without the class seeing what you have chosen.

2. Tell the pupils what you have done and ask them to show you which Shapes might be in the bag. Ask the pupils to tell you about which Shapes they choose, and check that they total 15.

3. Show one of the Shapes in the Feely Bag to the pupils and ask them to show or tell you what the remaining two Shapes might be. Again, check their addition.

4. Show them another of the Shapes and ask them what the last Shape in the Bag must be.

Repeat with three different Shapes.

Exploring combinations of numbers using three Numicon Shapes can take several different directions. The Shapes can all be different or all the same, or can be a pair the same and one other. The main part of this investigation is set out in two phases.

The Main Part: Phase 1

This part of the investigation focuses on the question:

'What are the smallest and largest totals of three shapes, and can all possible totals in between be made using three Shapes?'

Start by asking the pupils the following two questions:

'If I have only three shapes in the Feely Bag, what is the smallest number they could make? How about the largest?'

The answers to the above questions are of course 3 and 30 respectively, using three 1-shapes and three 10-shapes. Now ask:

'Can all totals between 3 and 30 be made with only three shapes?'

You might want to discuss with the pupils how they will record their solutions to this problem, e.g. as a sum or using Numicon Shapes.

Let the pupils work on their own for a time, then initiate a discussion about what they have found out. They might tell you any of the following:

That changing one Shape out of the three by a value of 1 will give a solution for the following number, i.e.

$2 + 5 + 7 = 14$

$3 + 5 + 7 = 15$

$4 + 5 + 7 = 16$, etc.

That some solutions are made using consecutive numbers, i.e.

$2 + 3 + 4 = 9$

That some solutions are made using multiples of the same number, i.e.

$5 + 5 + 5 = 15$

This phase comes to a natural conclusion when solutions for all numbers from 3 to 30 have been found. Now for the second phase.

The Main Part: Phase 2

This phase of the investigation focuses on the following question, which should be put to the class:

'Using three Numicon Shapes, how many ways can any number between 30 and 3 be made?'

Choose a particular number (numbers between 12 and 24 have lots of different solutions). Ask the pupils to combine three Shapes to make that number and record their answers. This is a good opportunity to work methodically. The pupils can work as a group, explore the numbers, and make a solution 'bank' of the permutations for each number. Take 12 as our example number.

The pupils may suggest:

1 + 1 + 10

1 + 2 + 9

1 + 3 + 8

1 + 4 + 7

They may also suggest possibilities:

1 + 5 + 6

2 + 2 + 8

2 + 3 + 7

2 + 4 + 6

2 + 5 + 5

3 + 3 + 6

3 + 4 + 5

4 + 4 + 4

Coincidentally, there are 12 possible solutions. Notice that working methodically allows all the solutions for a given number to be found. In this case we started with all the solutions that include 1. Next, look for all solutions including 2, being careful not to include a 1 in this list. Then find all solutions using 3 that do not include 1 or 2, etc.

Pupils can choose to explore any number from 3 to 30. They may come up with novel methods for finding all the possible solutions for their chosen number using these Shapes, which will provoke discussion.

What next?

After a time it will become apparent that some numbers have many solutions and some numbers have very few. Ask the pupils why some numbers have lots of possibilities and some have only a few and if there is a pattern to these results.

Plotting a graph showing the number of solutions for each total results in a bell curve as shown in figure 1.

Discuss with the children why the graph has the shape it does. Can they explain why there are only two solutions for the two smallest and two largest totals. Some children may be intrigued by the incremental increase shown in the graph and look back at their recording for reasons.

The limiting factor is that totals are only made using numbers (Numicon Shapes) 1-10. There are fewer solutions for the smallest and largest totals because the number of Shapes that can be used is limited. The totals in the middle of the range have the greatest number of solutions because a wider range of Shapes can be used to make these totals.

To extend the investigation you could also ask the class to consider the following questions:

'Find totals that can be made with consecutive numbers e.g.
3 + 4 + 5 = 12'

'Find totals that can be made using three numbers that are the same – is there a pattern in these totals?'

Figure 1

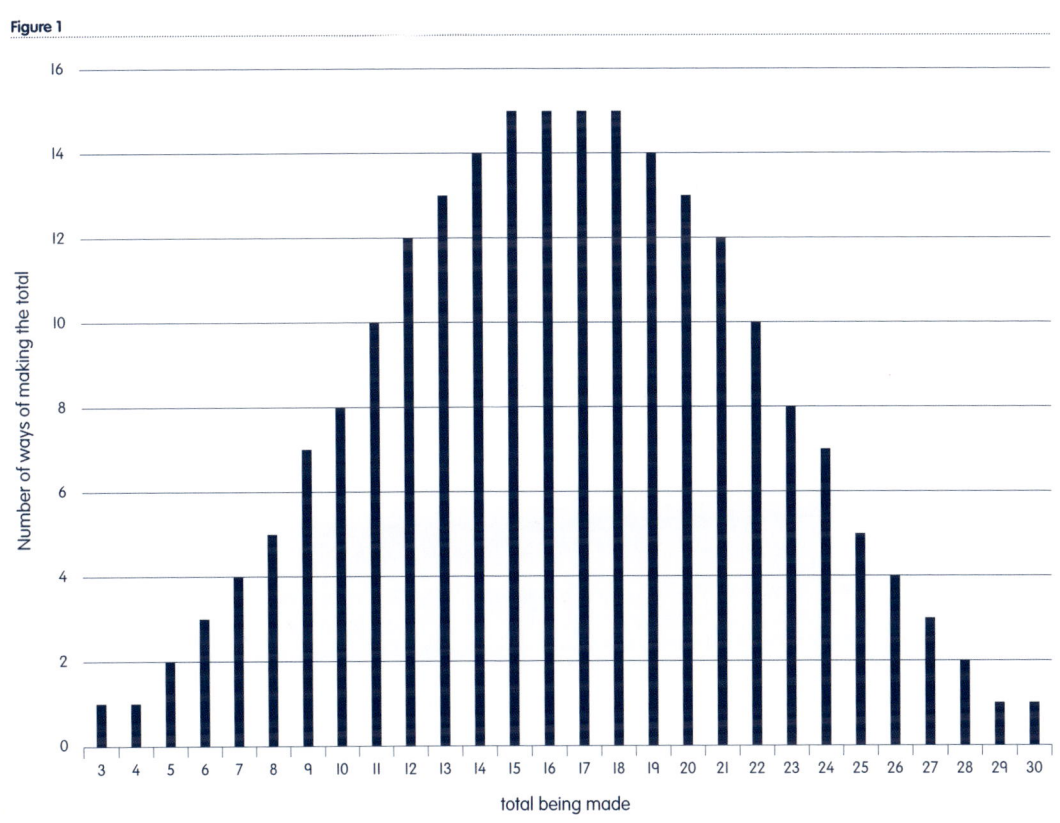

Magic Squares

Magic Squares have existed for centuries. They occur in a variety of places including the Lo Shu of Chinese mythology in 2800 BC. They were used by Arabian astrologers in the 9th century AD for drawing up horoscopes and in Albert Dürer's 'Melancholia I' where the date of the work, 1514, is in the bottom row of a 4 x 4 Magic Square.

You will need...
• Numicon Shapes
• Large sheets of paper with 3 x 3 grids, squares drawn to fit a Numicon 10-shape
• Paper and pencils

National Curriculum Attainment Targets
Ma2: 1a ,1b, 1d, 1i, 1k, 3d,

Starting Point

There is much opportunity for trial and improvement in this problem and some careful mathematical deduction regarding Magic Numbers. By working with Numicon Shapes pupils can physically manipulate the numbers in the Magic Square and simultaneously recognize their value, identifying rows, columns and diagonals that are clearly too large or too small.

Start by asking the pupils the following question:

'Can you take nine numbers and arrange them on a 3 x 3 grid so that the rows, columns and two diagonals all add up to the same number?'

Start with the simple version shown in figure 1, using three each of Numicon Shapes 1, 2, and 3. This will show the pupils how the problem works without their having to worry too much about the addition.

Pupils organize the Shapes onto a 3 x 3 grid, as described in the question.

'What number do all the rows, columns and diagonals have to add up to?'

In this example it is 6. This is the Magic Number.

'What is the link between the Magic Number and the Magic Square?'

This is a very important discussion to have with the class because it is much easier to solve a Magic Square if you know the Magic Number beforehand.

It is hoped that pupils will see that the Magic Number can be found by adding up all the numbers in the square and dividing this total by 3 in this case (the total is shared equally across three rows or columns). So, 18 divided by 3 is 6, which is the Magic Number. Figure 1 shows one possible solution completed with numbers and Numicon Shapes. If the pupils find different solutions, how do their's compare with the examples in figure 1?

Figure 1

3	1	2
1	2	3
2	3	1

The Main Part

Once they understand the nature of the problem, you can move on to the 1-9 Magic Square. The idea is the same, but the higher numbers make it more challenging.

'Can you arrange Numicon Shapes 1-9 in a 3 x 3 grid so that all the rows, columns and diagonals add up to the same number?'

A good idea is first to work out the Magic Number for this Magic Square. For help in solving this problem, shown in figure 2, refer back to the 1-2-3 Magic Square.

'Does the same rule for finding the Magic Number apply here?'

It does, so in this case 15 is the Magic Number for each row, column and diagonal i.e.

$1 + 2 + 3 + 4 + 5 + 6 + 7 + 8 + 9 = 45$

$45 \div 3 = 15$

Considerably more trial and improvement is involved here than for the previous problem.

What Next?

Once again, it is useful to look at a variety of solutions and find common links between them. Pupils may find:

• Solutions with reflective symmetry

• That the central number is 5. How does putting 5 in the middle help solve the problem? Is there a solution where 5 is not in the middle?

To give the pupils a more serious challenge ask them the following questions:

'Can a Magic Square be made up with any numbers? If not, what are the rules?'

The numbers do have to form some kind of pattern. If the 1-9 set is taken as a basis, then this set could be doubled, halved, subtracted from, added to, even multiplied by 100 and Magic Squares could still be made, albeit with different Magic Numbers.

'Can you make a Magic Square by placing the numbers 1-16 in a 4 x 4 square?'

Figure 3 shows one solution which can be used to give hints if pupils get stuck. Do pupils notice that not only do the rows, columns and diagonals add up to 34, any block of four squares also adds up to 34?

Figure 2

8	3	4
1	5	9
6	7	2

Figure 3

9	6	3	16
4	15	10	5
14	1	8	11
7	12	13	2

Sum and Product

The sum of two numbers is the number you get when you add them together; the product is the number you get when you multiply them together. 'Sum and Product' is a mathematical game that hones trial and improvement and multiplication and addition skills and develops logical thinking about number.

You will need...
- Numicon Shapes and/or Number Rods
- Numicon Tens Number Lines and/or Numicon Number Rod Tracks
- Feely Bag
- Pencil and paper
- Pinboard and drawing pins

National Curriculum Attainment Targets
Ma2: 1a ,1d, 1h, 1i, 1k, 2b, 3d, 3i

Starting Point

Note, It is essential that pupils try this investigation before doing 'Maximum', which comes later.

Without showing the class, choose two Numicon Shapes and put them in the Feely Bag. Tell the class what you have done and that they are going to have to work out which two Shapes are in the Bag. The clues are the **sum** of the two Shapes and the **product** of the two Shapes. Ask the question:

'There are two Shapes in the Feely Bag. The sum of the two Shapes is 9 and the product is 18. Using Numicon Shapes and pencil and paper can you work out which two Shapes are in the Bag?'

The Main Part

Now it is time for pupils to set problems for one another.* A key part of the strategy for finding out what Shapes are hidden is knowing the factors of the product. Pupils will either need to know factors of numbers to 30 (depending on their range of understanding) or the means of working them out. They will also need to be familiar with addition facts to 20 or have the means for working them out.

1. Using the Photocopy Master record sheet and working individually pupils calculate the sum and product of two Numicon Shapes chosen by themselves.

2. They enter this information on the left hand side of the record sheet, keeping the right hand side blank for others to complete the answers.

3. Ask pupils to put up their questions on the pin-board.

4. Pupils then choose problems to solve. They can use Number Rods and Numicon Shapes to find possible solutions.

If the sum is 12, the solution set would look like figure 1. If the product is 32 then each pair could be tested to find which gives this answer. Some pupils might wish to lay multiples of Numicon Shapes on a Tens Number Line or Number Rods in a track to check, as in figure 2.

At the end of the session the problem setters can reveal their Numicon Shapes and everyone can check their solutions.

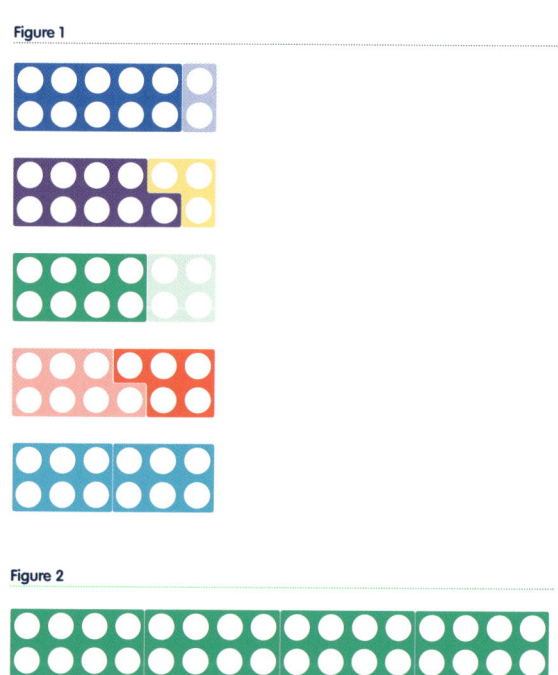

Figure 1

Figure 2

* Pupils will need access to the 'Sum and Product' Photocopy Master at the back of this booklet or available to download from the Numicon website:
http://www.numicon.com/numicon_free_resources/teaching-support-resources/resources_for_numicon_activities.html

What next?

How were solutions found? What trial and improvement techniques did pupils employ? Did they notice multiples of 5, of 10, or the odd and even multiplication rules, shown in figure 3? How might these observations help?

Discussing these rules will help with other problems.

This work can be made more difficult by moving the investigation into a purely number problem without using Numicon Shapes. Ask pupils to:

'Increase the size of the numbers used, e.g. try one number in the 1–10 range and one in the 11–20 range or use three numbers of less than 10.'

Figure 3

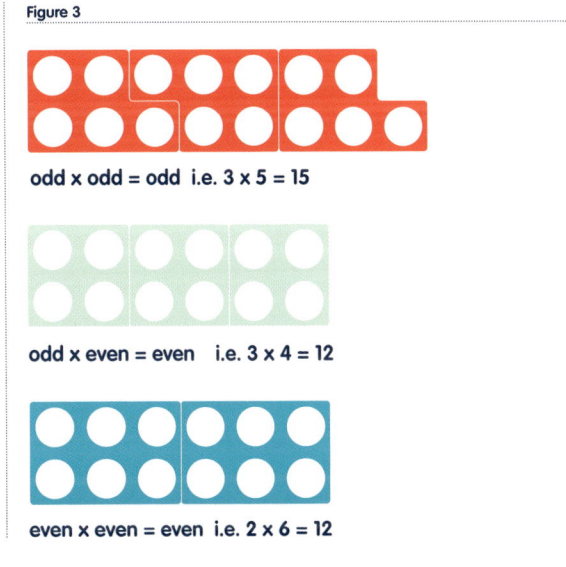

odd x odd = odd i.e. 3 x 5 = 15

odd x even = even   i.e. 3 x 4 = 12

even x even = even i.e. 2 x 6 = 12

Only Threes and Fives

Only Threes and Fives involves exercises using these two numbers only, and addition. By working in a structured way, pupils will see patterns emerging and be able to discuss what they have found.

You will need...
- Numicon Shapes
- Paper and pencils

National Curriculum Attainment Targets
Ma2: 1a ,1d, 1f, 1g, 1i, 1k

Starting Point

The principal idea is to find which totals can be made using Numicon 3-shapes and 5-shapes (or number rods). It is interesting first to look at the possible totals from each of these by recording them on a 100 square. Ask the question:

'If you had an unlimited supply of Numicon 3-shapes what totals could you make?'

Pupils could start by fitting the Shapes together and adding to find totals. Recording all the solutions on a hundred square creates a rather pleasing diagonal pattern, as shown in figure 1. This pattern emerges because the three times table has direct links with the nine times table. The 100 square is organized into rows of 10. Since 3 x 3 = 9 each new row will have a shaded square that is one down and one to the left of the shaded numbers in the rows above.

After a while, some pupils will abandon the apparatus when they see the pattern, just use mental addition to calculate the answers, or simply 'hop on' three spaces on the 100 square. Now ask the question:

'If you had an unlimited supply of Numicon 5-shapes what totals could you make?'

If the totals for 5s are recorded on the 100 square it will look like figure 2. The two columns are produced because of the relationship between 5 and 10 and because, as explained above, the 100 square is organized in rows of 10. Since 2 x 5 = 10 the shaded squares will always appear in columns.

Having found these solutions we can explore what happens when the two numbers (three and five) are combined.

Figure 1

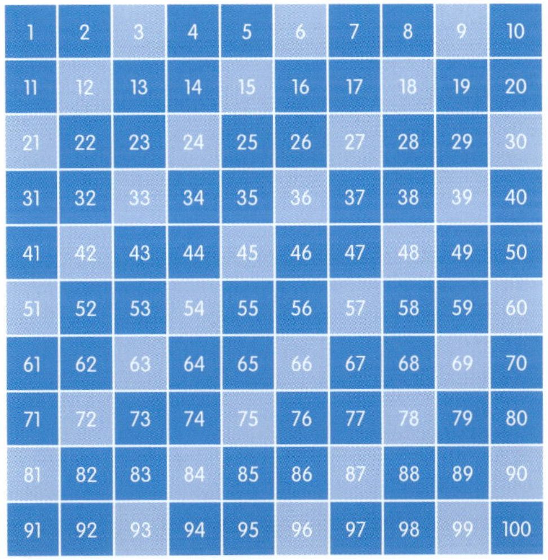

Figure 2

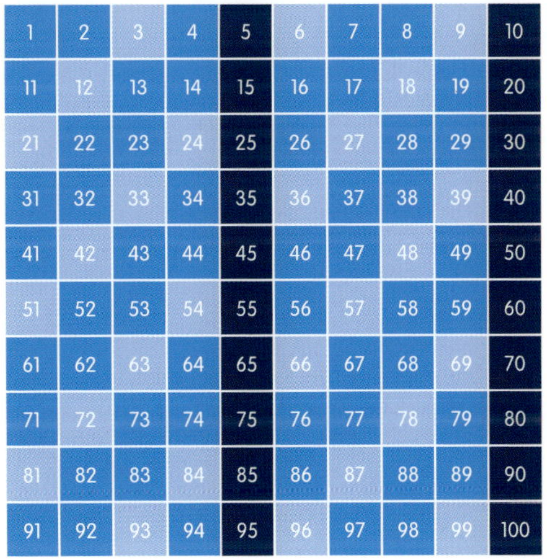

The Main Part

Ask the question:

'Of the remaining numbers in the 100 square in figure 2, how many can be made by combining 3s and 5s?'

If pupils try the remaining numbers in order, because there are so few possible combinations of 3 and 5 they will quickly realize you cannot make 1, 2, 4 and 7. Once they get to 8, 9 and 10 they will find all the other numbers can be made:

$5 + 3 = 8$

$3 + 3 + 3 = 9$

$5 + 5 = 10$

Once they have three consecutive totals then the next three build on them:

$5 + 3 + 3 = 11$

$3 + 3 + 3 + 3 = 12$

$5 + 5 + 3 = 13$

Continuing to add 3 to each of these strings gives the next three totals and so on. This rule is important as later the investigation can be developed further to explore other pairs of numbers that add up to 8. Does this type of rule still hold for these new pairs?

Once pupils have got to this stage you can show them how to record their answers in a more efficient way. It would be unwieldy to write some of the larger solutions in only 3s and 5s, but using multiples and brackets makes it manageable.

For example, 88 is 17 fives and 1 three, which can be written as:

$(17 \times 5) + 3 = 88$

Which is much more efficient than:

$5 + 5 + 5 + 5 + 5 + 5 + 5 + 5 + 5 + 5 + 5 + 5 + 5 + 5 + 5 + 5 + 5 + 3 = 88$

What next?

When all possible solutions on the 100 square have been found you can discuss the following questions:

What solutions can be made with other pairs of numbers that add up to 8?

Is there a better way of splitting the number so more solutions can be found?

Can some solutions be made in more than one way?

If you choose another pair of numbers, e.g. 3 and 7, how many solutions on the 100 square can be made?

What happens when you have a pair of even numbers?

In this last situation, only even solutions can be made, whereas with two odds, or an odd and even pair, both odd and even solutions can be made.

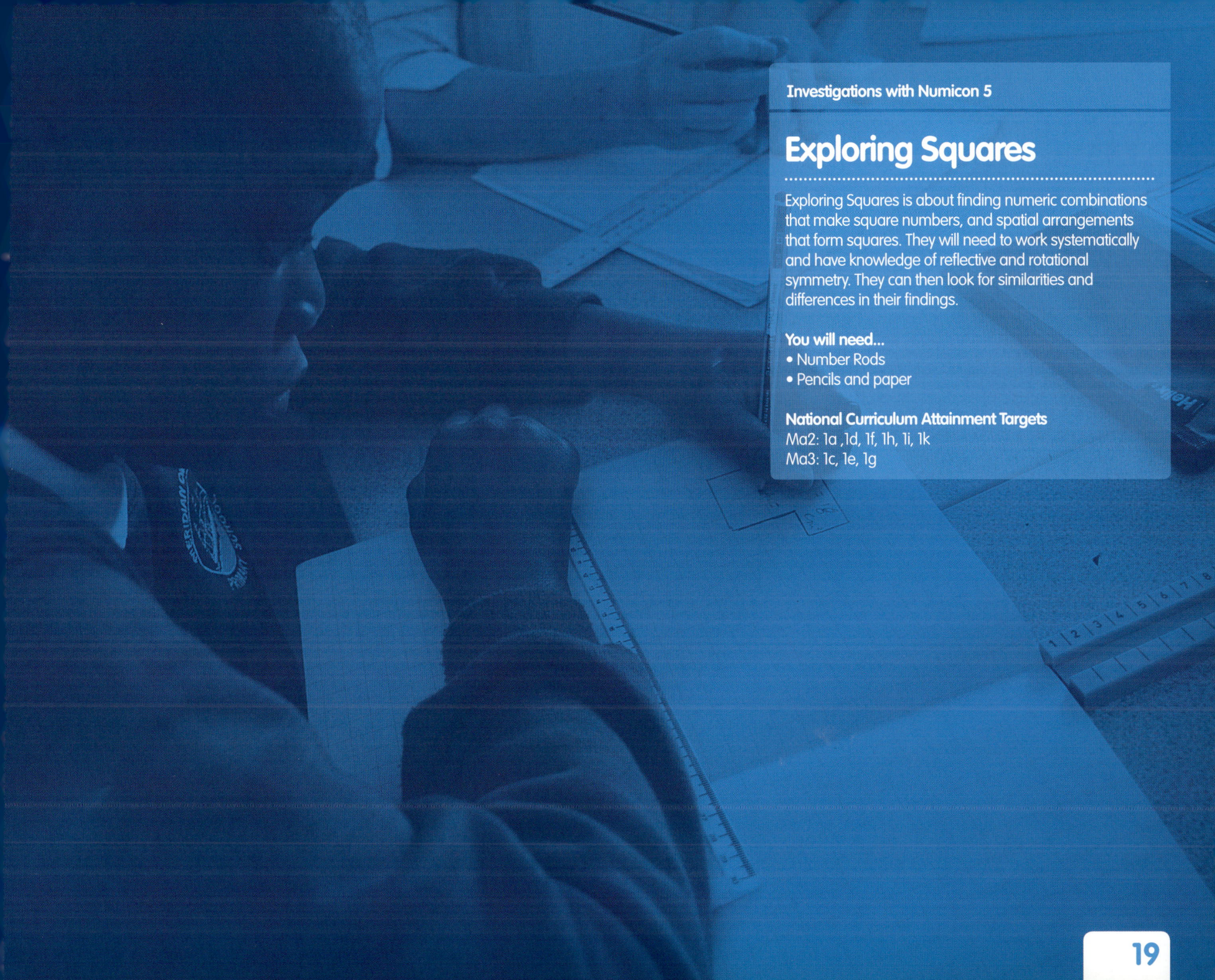

Exploring Squares

Exploring Squares is about finding numeric combinations that make square numbers, and spatial arrangements that form squares. They will need to work systematically and have knowledge of reflective and rotational symmetry. They can then look for similarities and differences in their findings.

You will need...
- Number Rods
- Pencils and paper

National Curriculum Attainment Targets
Ma2: 1a ,1d, 1f, 1h, 1i, 1k
Ma3: 1c, 1e, 1g

Starting Point

Ask the question:

Using the Number Rods how many ways can you make a 2 x 2 square?

The solutions might look something like figure 1.

What emerges from their solutions for discussion?

Can solutions be grouped in other ways?

For example:

- sets of solutions that are re-arrangements of each other, some are rotated or reflected, see figures 1a to 1d.

- there is a core group of solutions on which all other re-arrangements are based. They will look something like figure 1 and can be expressed numerically as:

  $1 + 1 + 1 + 1 = 4$ figure 1a

  $1 + 1 + 2 = 4$ figure 1b rotated to make 1c

  $2 + 2 = 4$ figure 1d

Do pupils agree or disagree with how solutions can be made? Some might see a rotation as an acceptable solution; others might see it as a copy. It will make an interesting debate.

The Main Part

Now progress to a 3 x 3 square, either as an investigation of a 'core group' or of how one solution can take many forms through rearrangement or reflective or rotational symmetry.

In either case, finding all possible solutions will require pupils to work systematically and find a way to record their answers. They can compare their solutions to the numeric expressions.

A Core Group

Pupils are looking for a set of solutions that use a unique set of Number Rods. Rotations, reflections and rearrangements are not allowed. The three examples (figure 2 a,c,e overleaf) could be part of the core group solutions.

How can the arrangements in Figure 2 be recorded? As an addition sum, Figure 2a would be:

$3 + 2 + 2 + 1 + 1$ or $3 + 2 \times 2 + 2 \times 1$

However, this may prove confusing since it is not clear what the digits represent. Using brackets and some rules about which digits represent quantities and Number Rods, could help:

$3 + (2 \times 2) + (2 \times 1)$

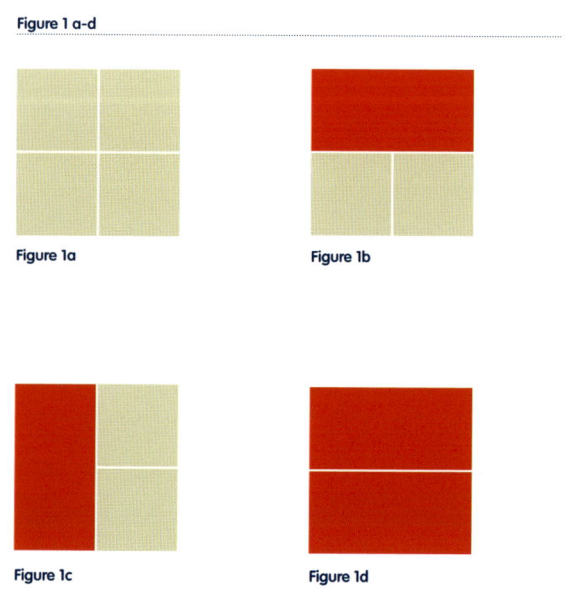

Figure 1 a-d

Figure 1a

Figure 1b

Figure 1c

Figure 1d

Here, the digits on their own are single Rods, the first digit in a bracket is the number of rods and the second is the rod value. Which means figure 2e would read like this:

3 + 2 + (4 x 1)

Ask the question:

How many core solutions are there for the 3 x 3 square?

Using Rotation, Reflection and Rearrangement
In this case, a core solution can be manipulated into many alternatives. The number of alternatives depends on the variety and number of individual pieces that make up the square and the type of manipulation. Some pupils will only rearrange the shapes or use reflective symmetry.

This is a much more open-ended exercise than the previous exploration and will demand systematic organization and recording in order to find every possible solution.

What next?

Since much of this work is pictorial, pupils may want to explore and then display their findings. They could work in groups to make a presentation.

Exploring the 4 x 4 square greatly extends the scope of the investigation.

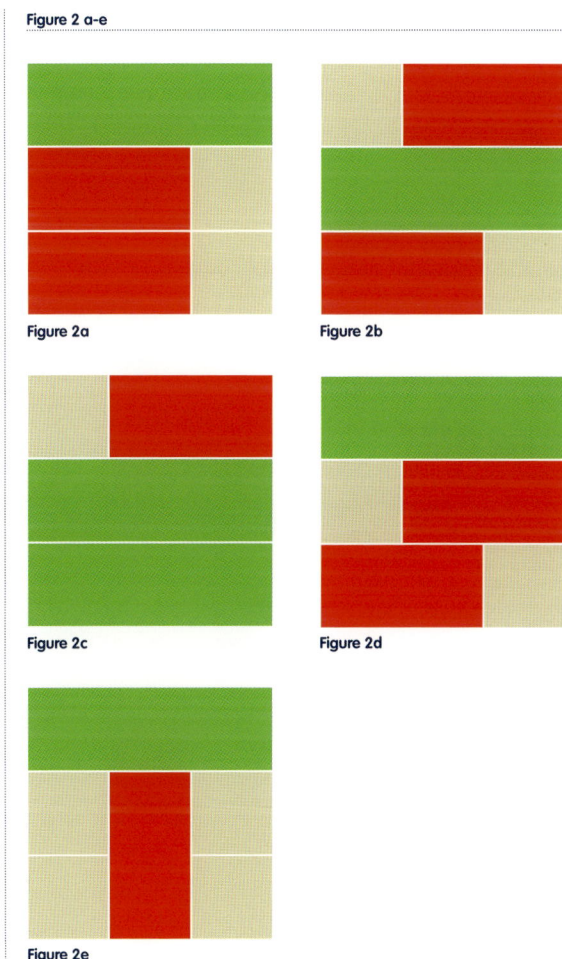

Figure 2 a-e

Figure 2a

Figure 2b

Figure 2c

Figure 2d

Figure 2e

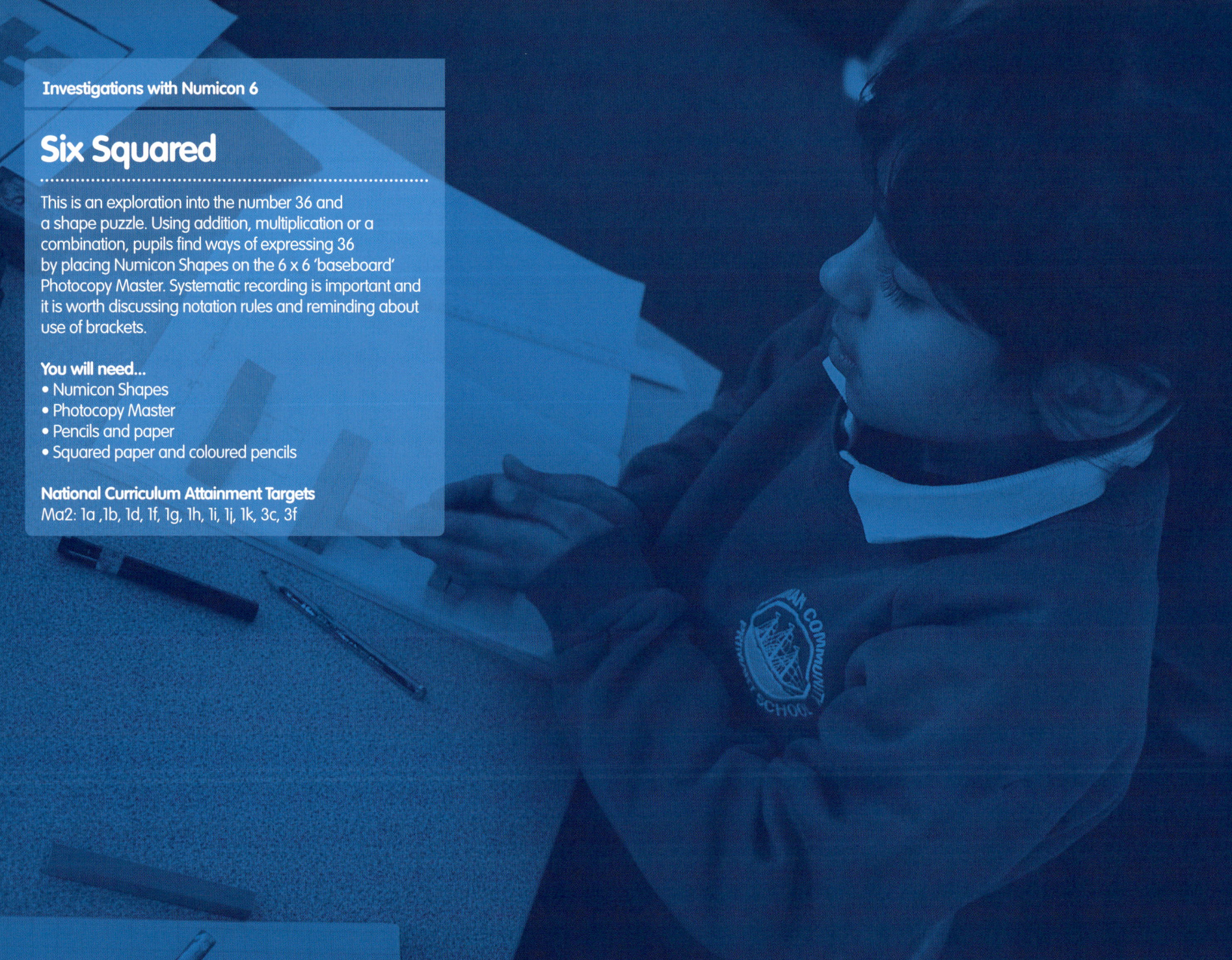

Six Squared

This is an exploration into the number 36 and
a shape puzzle. Using addition, multiplication or a
combination, pupils find ways of expressing 36
by placing Numicon Shapes on the 6 x 6 'baseboard'
Photocopy Master. Systematic recording is important and
it is worth discussing notation rules and reminding about
use of brackets.

You will need...
• Numicon Shapes
• Photocopy Master
• Pencils and paper
• Squared paper and coloured pencils

National Curriculum Attainment Targets
Ma2: 1a ,1b, 1d, 1f, 1g, 1h, 1i, 1j, 1k, 3c, 3f

Starting Point

Pupils should work with the 6 x 6 'baseboard' Photocopy Master.* Describe the activity:

'Explore the square by filling it with Numicon Shapes of your choice, then decide how to record what you have found.'

Discuss how multiples of one Shape might be recorded as a sum, for example the layout in figure 1 could be recorded as:

10 + 2 + 8 + 8 + 4 + 4 = 36

or

10 + 2 + 2 x 8 + 2 x 4 = 36

Some pupils may find this confusing and may understand better if you use brackets, i.e.

10 + 2 + (2 x 8) + (2 x 4) = 36

It is useful to decide on the order of the numbers in the brackets. The first number could be the quantity of the Shape used and the second the Shape value.

The Main Part

This investigation into the number 36 moves into a series of challenges. In each case it is important for pupils to be systematic about recording their findings.

1. Fill the 6 x 6 'baseboard' only with Numicon Shapes of values of 5 and over, or 6 and over, etc. Figure 2 depicts one solution.

2. How many ways is it possible to fill the square using only one of any Shape value? Figure 3 depicts one solution.

3. How can the board be filled with only one type of Shape? Figure 4 shows a solution using only Numicon 4-shapes.

4. Using only two different Shapes, show as many ways as possible of covering the 6 x 6 'baseboard'. Figures 5 and 6 show solutions using only Numicon 2- and 6-shapes.

5. What is the smallest number of Shapes needed to cover the 6 x 6 'baseboard'? Find as many combinations as possible and record the answers. When pupils find the smallest number of Shapes is five (see figure 7) ask why it could not be four.

6. Individually pupils could organize five Shapes on to the 6 x 6 'baseboard', record their solution, and challenge their partner to fit the same five Shapes on to the board. Is there more than one solution?

Figure 1

* Pupils will need access to the 'Sum and Product' Photocopy Master at the back of this booklet or available to download from the Numicon website: http://www.numicon.com/numicon_free_resources/teaching-support-resources/resources_for_numicon_activities.html

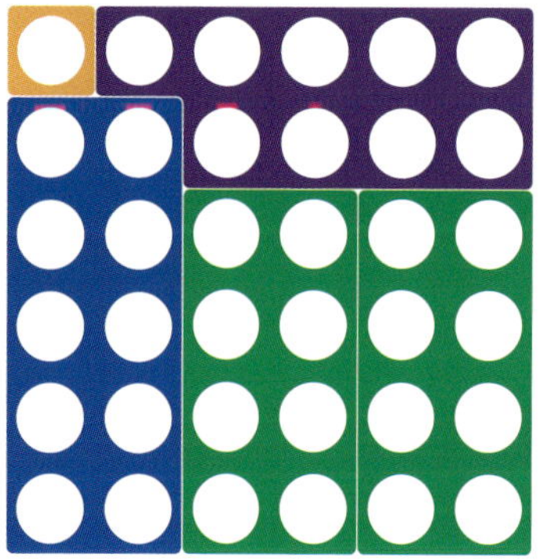

What next?

At the end of each task, review the findings in a group. Ask the following questions:

How many ways did you find?

Was anything impossible, e.g. fitting four 9-Shapes into a 6 x 6 square?

Which part of the investigation did you enjoy the most? Was this because it was the most difficult?

Figure 2

Figure 3

Figure 4

Figure 5

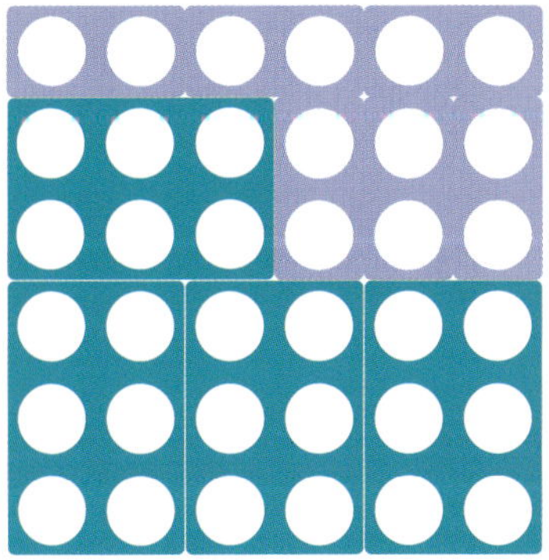

Figure 6

Figure 7

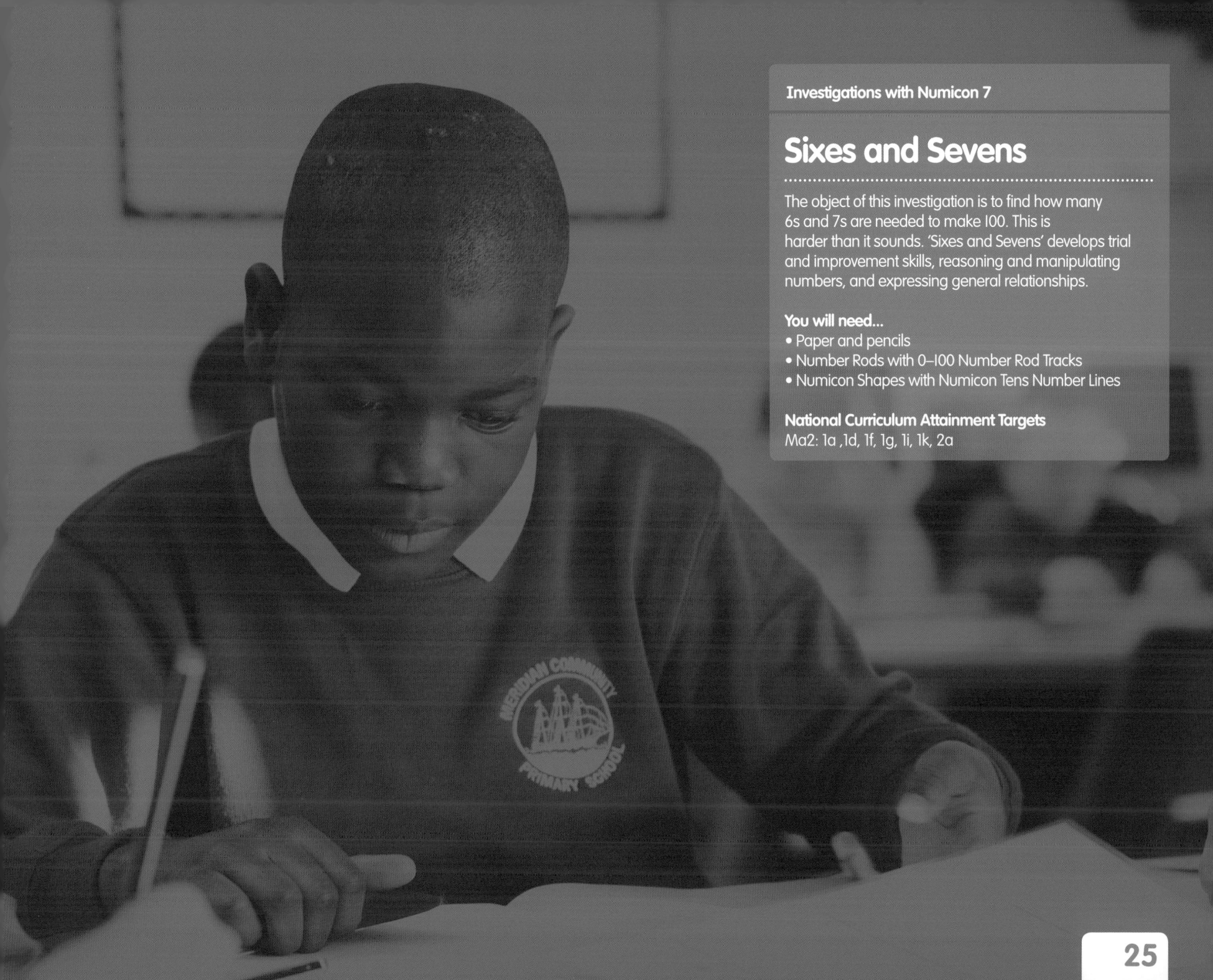

Sixes and Sevens

The object of this investigation is to find how many 6s and 7s are needed to make 100. This is harder than it sounds. 'Sixes and Sevens' develops trial and improvement skills, reasoning and manipulating numbers, and expressing general relationships.

You will need...
- Paper and pencils
- Number Rods with 0–100 Number Rod Tracks
- Numicon Shapes with Numicon Tens Number Lines

National Curriculum Attainment Targets
Ma2: 1a ,1d, 1f, 1g, 1i, 1k, 2a

Starting Point

Ask one of the following questions depending on the resources you are using:

'Using only the 6 and 7 Number Rods on the 0-100 Number Rod Track is it possible to make 100?' or

'Can Numicon 6- and 7-shapes be laid in a line that totals 100?'

Using their supply of Numicon Shapes or apparatus the pupils can try out and refine combinations of these two numbers until they reach their goal.

How do pupils express their answers?

As multiple addition:

6 + 6 + 6 + 6 + 6 + 7 + 7 + 7 + 7 + 7 + 7 + 7 + 7 + 7 + 7 = 100

In words:

'You need five sixes and ten sevens to make one hundred.'

Using multiplication and addition:

5 x 6 = 30   10 x 7 = 70   giving   30 + 70 = 100

Then you could ask them if 100 can be made in more than one way, i.e:

12 x 6 = 72   4 x 7 = 28   giving   72 + 28 = 100

The Main Part

This investigation can be broadened.

Instead of 6s and 7s, what other pairs of numbers from 2 to 9 will combine to total 100? Are there pairs that will not work? This question is important because it will motivate some pupils to try to find pairs that do not.

At this stage they may choose to abandon the apparatus and work with pencil and paper, to write down the multiples of each number. Here are examples using 5s and 7s:

5, 10, 15, 20, 25, 30, 35, 40, 45, 50, 55, 60, 65, 70, 75, 80, 85, 90, 95, 100

7, 14, 21, 28, 35, 42, 49, 56, 63, 70, 77, 84, 91, 98

They can search for pairs of numbers that total 100.

What next?

In the course of the investigation pupils will probably identify some general rules. You should discuss these with the group. They might include:

It is always possible to make 100 when 2 is combined with another number.

Does this also work with 5?

Why do smaller number value pairs have more solutions than larger number pairs?

Do odd/odd, even/odd or even/even pairings make a difference to the number of possible solutions?

What is the smallest value pair of numbers that does not work?

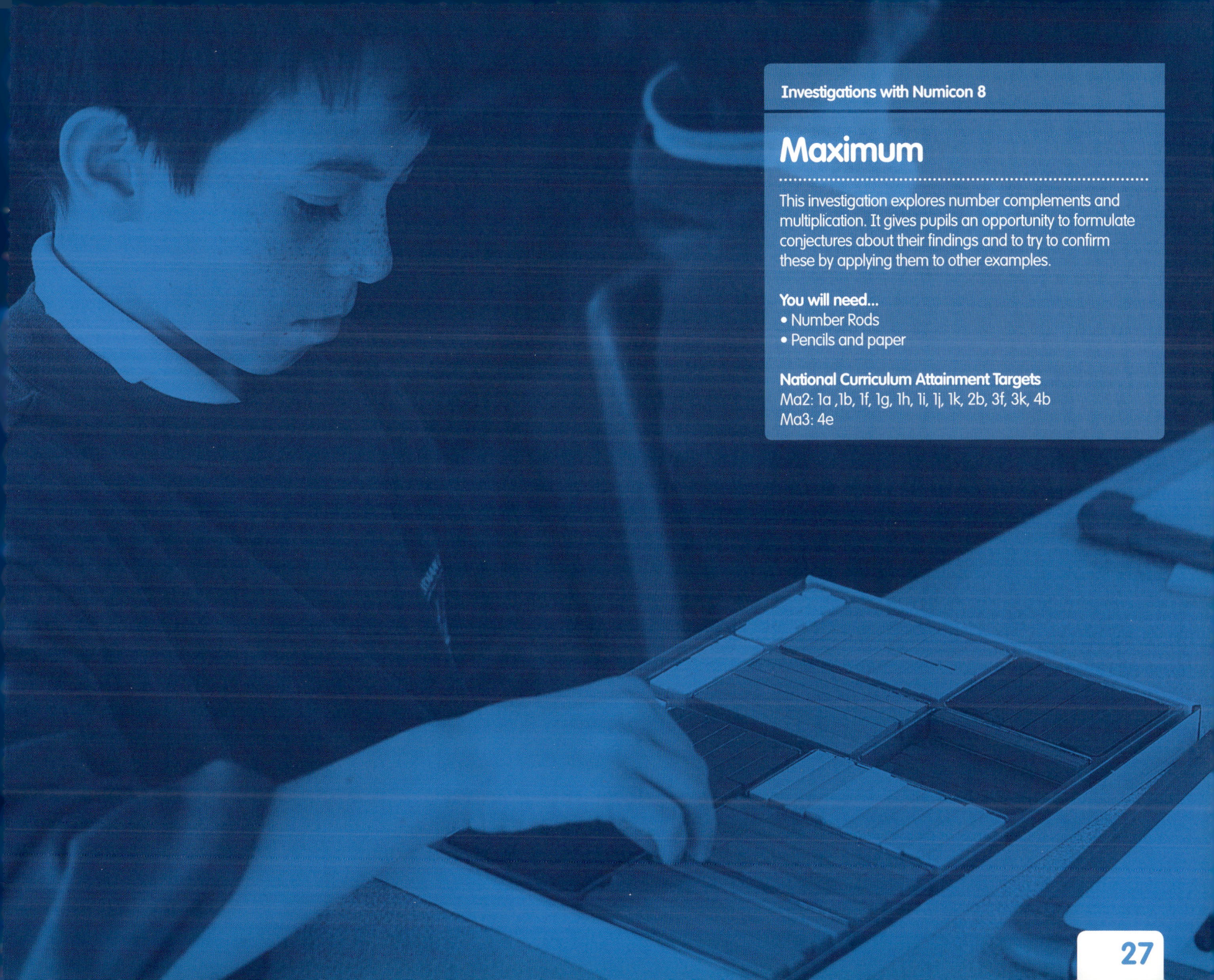

Maximum

This investigation explores number complements and multiplication. It gives pupils an opportunity to formulate conjectures about their findings and to try to confirm these by applying them to other examples.

You will need...
• Number Rods
• Pencils and paper

National Curriculum Attainment Targets
Ma2: 1a ,1b, 1f, 1g, 1h, 1i, 1j, 1k, 2b, 3f, 3k, 4b
Ma3: 4e

Starting Point

This investigation should only be attempted when 'Sum and Product' has been explored.

Start by asking:

'How many ways can sets of Number Rods be organized into rectangles so that the length of the rectangle plus the width of the rectangle equals 10?'

Ask the pupils to record their answers. There are 9 possible solutions, which are shown in figure 1.
Then ask:

'Which arrangement of rods gives the rectangle with the biggest area?'

In answering this question the pupils could form a conjecture or an unproven idea. They might, for example, state, "When the length and width are the same the area is maximum." One element of the next stage of the investigation sets out to find if this is true.

The Main Part

Start by asking the pupils to do the following:

'Choose a whole number between 11 and 20. Split it into two parts. Make each either the length or width of a rectangle. Which combination would result in the shape with the greatest area?'

How does this relate to the conjecture formulated in the starting point?

Is the conjecture true for any number between 11 and 20?

Gather the pupils' findings to see what they have discovered about different numbers. Check that the children have noticed the following:

When the length plus the width equals an even number, the maximum area occurs when both of these are equal, i.e. the shape is a square.

When the length plus width make an odd number the maximum area occurs when the length and width differ by 1.

This investigation opens up considerably if the numbers are split into more than three parts, which creates three dimensional shapes. Some pupils may find it helpful to visualize three dimensional shapes by building them with Number Rods, others may find drawing them a helpful support, while others may just work numerically.

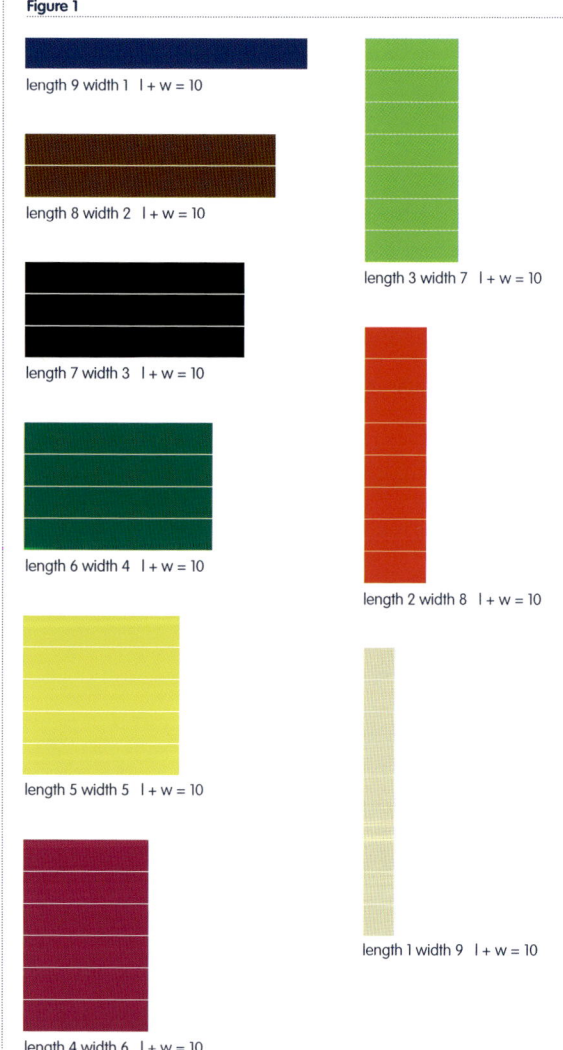

Figure 1

length 9 width 1 l + w = 10

length 8 width 2 l + w = 10

length 7 width 3 l + w = 10

length 6 width 4 l + w = 10

length 5 width 5 l + w = 10

length 4 width 6 l + w = 10

length 3 width 7 l + w = 10

length 2 width 8 l + w = 10

length 1 width 9 l + w = 10

What Next?

So ask the question:

Is it possible to make a shape with a bigger total?

Splitting the number into three parts will of course result in a cuboid being formed so the three numbers give a length, a width and a height, the result of l x w x h is volume. As mentioned on the previous page the volume of the cuboid could be represented using Number Rods.

Splitting a number into more than three parts would result shapes of four or more dimensions. This moves the investigation away from shape and into a purely numeric investigation.

Try breaking down the numbers into more parts. As the number of parts increases much larger numbers will be generated. Here are some totals gained when 15 is split into 3, 4 and 5 parts:

4 x 5 x 6 = 120

3 x 3 x 4 x 5 = 180

2 x 2 x 3 x 4 x 4 = 192

Now ask the question:

What number combinations result in highest products? What about the lowest?

The highest products will result from combinations of 2s and 3s. There is a limit to the number of splits that yield increasingly large results since if 1 is used as the multiplier, it has no effect on the answers. Discuss with the class how the findings relate to the conjecture formulated in the starting point.

Explore using decimals. Arithmetically this is more complex and may require the use of calculators.

Again, using 15 as an example, we can break it down into:

7 + 8 = 15 giving the product 7 x 8 = 56

or

7.5 + 7.5 = 15 giving the product 7.5 x 7.5 = 56.25

This may lead to a much deeper exploration of maximum products for instance using two, three or more decimal places. Discuss how the findings relate to the conjecture formulated in the starting point.

Consecutive Numbers

Numicon Shapes are ideal for this investigation as they fall elegantly into consecutive patterns. 'Consecutive Numbers' explores important fundamentals of number, including odds and evens, addition, division and powers of 2. In the course of the investigation, pupils will see the advantage of setting out their work systematically to reveal patterns.

You will need...
• Numicon Shapes
• Paper and pencils

National Curriculum Attainment Targets
Ma2: 1a ,1d, 1f, 1i, 1j, 1k, 2b, 3d, 3f, 3h

Starting Point

Start by asking:

'Using the Numicon Shapes from 1 to 10, what totals are found when adding two consecutive numbers?'

Here is the solution:

$1 + 2 = 3$

$2 + 3 = 5$

$3 + 4 = 7$

$4 + 5 = 9$

$5 + 6 = 11$

$6 + 7 = 13$

$7 + 8 = 15$

$8 + 9 = 17$

$9 + 10 = 19$

Organizing the totals in order reveals the pattern of odd numbers after the equals sign and the two columns of consecutive numbers before the equals sign. The pattern of odd numbers is significant and leads into the main part of the investigation.

The Main Part

Question the pupils about what they have found. Once they recognize the odd number pattern ask:

'Why are all the totals odd?'

Rules of addition state that:

odd + odd = even

odd + even = odd

even + even = even

Since consecutive numbers fall into the odd-even, even-odd pattern, adding two consecutive numbers will always give an odd total.

Suggest that the pupils might like to use more than two Numicon Shapes.

'So, what happens if you add more than two consecutive numbers, what other totals can be made?'

Here are some examples

$1 + 2 + 3 = 6$

$1 + 2 + 3 + 4 = 10$

$3 + 4 + 5 = 12$

Start to refer to a 'string' of consecutive numbers, as this term is used later in the investigation.

You can ask the following questions to act as discussion points to take this investigation further.

'Can you predict whether totalling a string of three or more consecutive numbers will result in an odd or even total?'

'Can different strings of consecutive numbers give the same total?'

For example, 9 is '2-stringed' because it can be made in two ways using consecutive numbers:

$4 + 5 = 9$ and $2 + 3 + 4 = 9$

What next?

Which numbers have the most strings?

This question leads to a much deeper exploration and may be accessible only to more able mathematicians at the top of the primary school. It does require pupils to have some knowledge of number patterns (e.g. primes, squares). Ask pupils to find all the strings for numbers up to thirty and then start to look for patterns in the numbers with different numbers of 'strings'. Using these patterns, ideas can be developed, discussed and conjectures formed for proof by example. Here are a few ideas about what might emerge or could be hinted at for exploration:

• Prime numbers only ever have one string. The other one-stringed numbers are primes multiplied by the power of 2.

• Most numbers in the 3 times table can be made using a string of three numbers (similarly for the 5 times table, etc.)

• All numbers that are squares but not powers of 2 are 2-stringed.

Discuss and explore findings and ideas.

The most able mathematicians at the top of the primary school might wish to take this further to explore the relationship between the factors of a number and its strings, e.g. some numbers in the three times table are made of a string of three numbers. Does this idea work for any other numbers?

For any given number is it possible to devise methods for finding strings of consecutive numbers that add up to it?

The numbers that cannot be made with a string of consecutive numbers are the powers of 2, i.e. 2, 4, 8, 16, 32, 64, etc.

The reason is complex and involves a mathematical 'proof by contradiction', but the idea can be explored as shown below:

For example, 2 cannot be made from a string of consecutive numbers; the smallest number constituting a string is 3, i.e. 1 + 2.

Four is also a problem. 1 + 2 = 3 and 2 + 3 = 5. There are no other ways of combining consecutive numbers smaller than four to make this number.

This does not prove that no power of 2 cannot be made from a string of consecutive numbers, but it provokes some mathematical debate. For example, is it true for 8? What about 16?

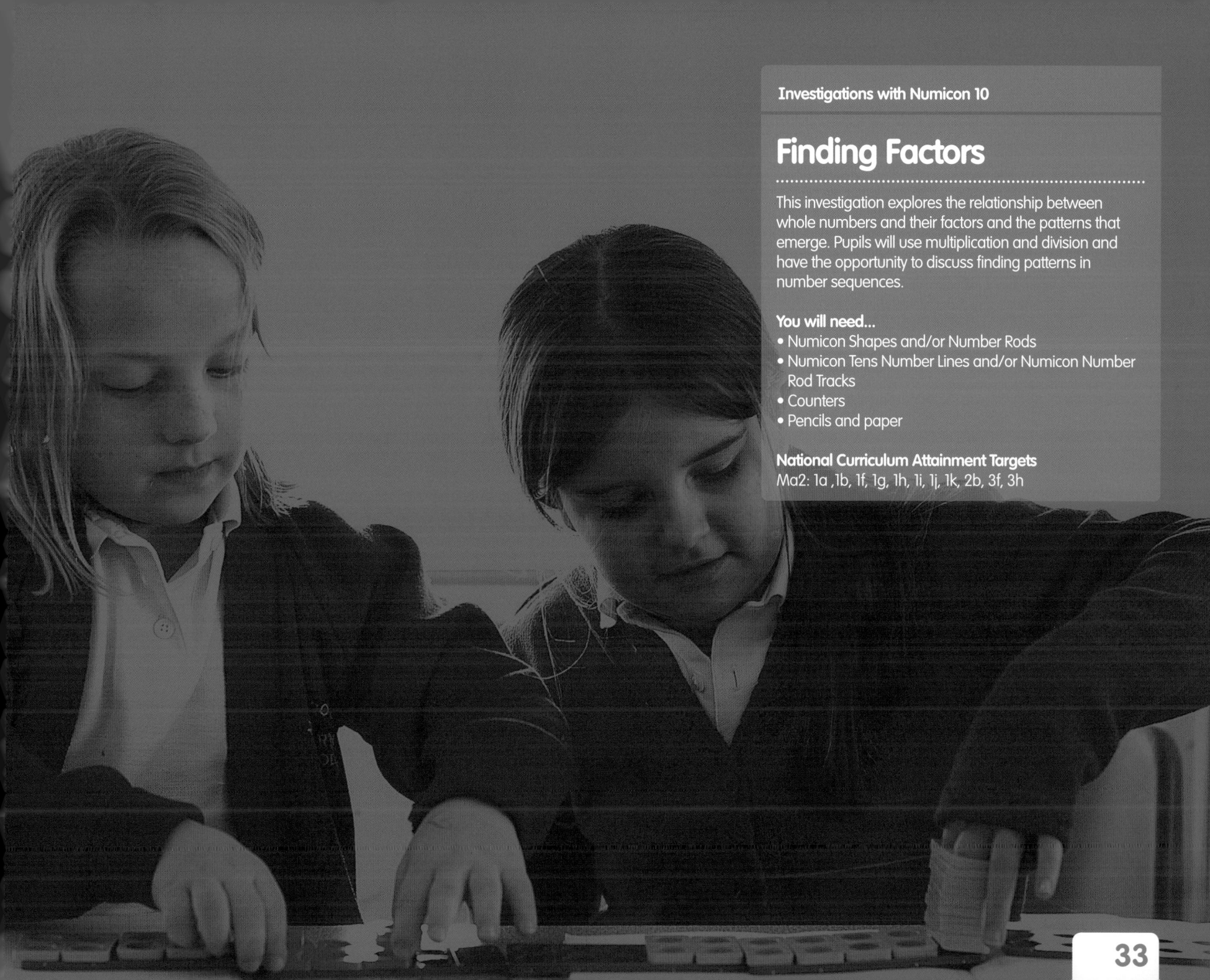

Finding Factors

This investigation explores the relationship between whole numbers and their factors and the patterns that emerge. Pupils will use multiplication and division and have the opportunity to discuss finding patterns in number sequences.

You will need...
- Numicon Shapes and/or Number Rods
- Numicon Tens Number Lines and/or Numicon Number Rod Tracks
- Counters
- Pencils and paper

National Curriculum Attainment Targets
Ma2: 1a ,1b, 1f, 1g, 1h, 1i, 1j, 1k, 2b, 3f, 3h

Starting Point

Ask the question:

'Using counters, or Number Rods, how many ways can 12 be formed into a rectangle?'

Figure 1 shows the options. The six numbers that describe the sides of the rectangles are called factors. The factors of twelve are 1, 2, 3, 4, 6 and 12.

The Main Part

This exercise has two objectives. First, gathering the factors of each number; second classifying the types of numbers that have been found. Ask the question:

'Can you find the factors of all numbers from 1 to 30?'

The pupils can choose to work from 1 to 30 or pick numbers randomly from the set. They can form rectangles using counters to find the factors, see examples in figure 1. Alternatively use Numicon Shapes on the Tens Number Line or number rods in the Number Rod Track.

Bring the class together to collate their findings which should look like the list in figure 2. When the table is complete for the numbers to 30, start to gather general information from the class about what they found. This might include:

- Some numbers have only two factors.

- Some numbers have lots of factors.

- 1, 4, 9, 16 and 25 have odd numbers of factors.

- Some small numbers may have more factors than some larger ones.

Five types of number can be identified from their factors. Introduce the number definitions below.

Square numbers
These have an odd number of factors. Look at Figure 3 which shows the factors of 16. Factors almost always work in pairs, but the factor 4 does not have a partner because its partner is itself. This attribute of having an odd number of factors applies to all square numbers.

Figure 1

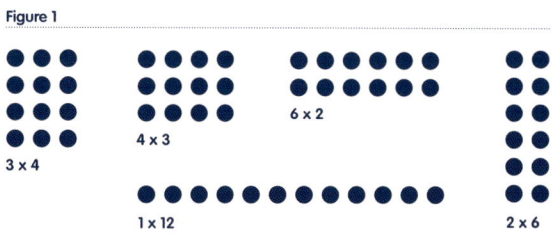

3 x 4 4 x 3 6 x 2
1 x 12 2 x 6

Figure 2

Number	Factors
1	1
2	1, 2
3	1, 3
4	1, 2, 4
5	1, 5
6	1, 2, 3, 6
7	1, 7
8	1, 2, 4, 8
9	1, 3, 9
10	1, 2, 5, 10
11	1, 11
12	1, 2, 3, 4, 6, 12
13	1, 13
14	1, 2, 7, 14
15	1, 3, 5, 15
16	1, 2, 4, 8, 16
17	1, 17
18	1, 2, 3, 6, 9, 18
19	1, 19
20	1, 2, 4, 5, 10, 20
21	1, 3, 7, 21
22	1, 2, 11, 22
23	1, 23
24	1, 2, 3, 4, 6, 8, 12, 24
25	1, 5, 25
26	1, 2, 13, 26
27	1, 3, 9, 27
28	1, 2, 4, 7, 14, 28
29	1, 29
30	1, 2, 3, 5, 6, 10, 15, 30

Prime numbers

These have exactly two factors, 1 and the number itself. Eleven, for example, can only be arranged as in figure 4.

Abundant numbers

If the sum of the factors is more than twice the number itself, it is called an abundant number. Adding up the factors of 20 (see list in figure 2 above) gives 42, so 20 is abundant since 42 > 2 x 20.

Deficient numbers

If the sum of the factors is less than twice the number itself, it is a deficient number. Most numbers are deficient – again check the list in figure 2.

Perfect numbers

If the sum of the numbers is exactly twice the number itself it is called perfect. There are very few perfect numbers, but the first two (6 and 28) are to be found in the table shown in figure 2.

'Can you sort the numbers according to their definition and identify any patterns?'

More Information About Sets of Numbers

In order to discuss the properties of numbers more fully The following explanations will help.

Square numbers

Some examples of square numbers are 1, 4, 9, 16, 25. They are called square numbers because the number of units that make them up can be arranged into a square.

'How does the sequence of square numbers grow?'

It helps to look at this pictorially by building the squares with number rods.

Each new square builds on the previous one by extending the length and width by one unit and this increases the number of new squares by the next number in the odd number sequence. So, any square number can be found by adding consecutive odd numbers starting with 1, see figure 5.

The same sequence can be found by looking at the 'first difference' of this pattern. To find a first difference, look at neighboring numbers. In the example below we could look at 1, 4. Subtracting 1 from 4 gives three, so 3 is the first difference. Next is 4, 9. 9 – 4 = 5 so 5 is the first difference of this pair. The set of first differences for this sequence looks like this:

Prime numbers

A prime number can only be divided by 1 and itself to give a whole number answer, so a prime number can be defined as having exactly two factors. Note, 1 is not a prime number; it has only one factor. The first few prime numbers are:

2, 3, 5, 7, 11, 13, 17, 19, 23, 29…

Searching for patterns within prime numbers has confounded mathematicians throughout the centuries.

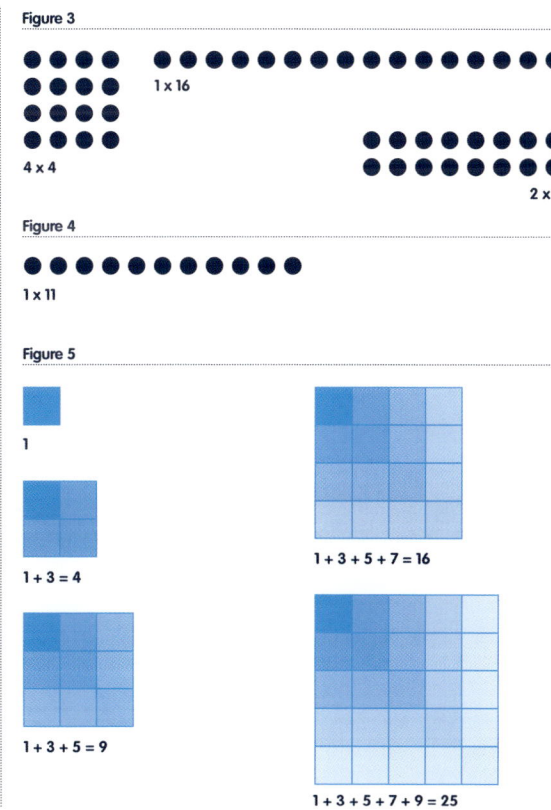

Figure 3

1 x 16

4 x 4

2 x 8

Figure 4

1 x 11

Figure 5

1

1 + 3 = 4

1 + 3 + 5 = 9

1 + 3 + 5 + 7 = 16

1 + 3 + 5 + 7 + 9 = 25

For example, with 'first differences' (shown above), the numbers 'jump' about and do not 'settle'. There are, however, some ways to organize the numbers and some rules that can be identified.

Ask the pupils to try the following:

'If you put the numbers 1-32 in four columns so the first row is 1-4, where do the prime numbers lie?'

All except two prime numbers are either one more or one fewer than a multiple of 4. Now ask the pupils:

'If you put numbers 1-30 into six columns so the first row is 1-6 ,where do the prime numbers lie? What does this demonstrate about prime numbers?'

Except for 2 and 3, the prime numbers are either one more or one fewer than a multiple of 6.

However, neither of these 'rules' for finding prime numbers works for all multiples of 4 and 6.

The Sieve of Eratosthenes

There is an intriguing and simple way to find all the prime numbers up to 100, using what is called the 'Sieve of Eratosthenes'. Eratosthenes was an Ancient Greek, a scholar (born AD 276) who developed a simple method for finding prime numbers. His sieve works by removing multiples of numbers whilst leaving the prime numbers behind.

Using the The Sieve of Eratosthenes Photocopy Master either demonstrate the following or ask each pupil to complete the following exercise:

Cross out 1, it is not a prime.

Circle 2, cross out all the multiples of 2 except 2.

Circle 3, cross out all the multiples of 3 except 3.

Circle the next un-shaded number and then cross out its multiples.

Keep going. How soon can you be sure you have found all the prime numbers in the 100 square?

All the circled numbers are prime numbers as shown in figure 2.

Abundant, Deficient and Perfect Numbers

Look at the list in figure 2 on page 34 and apply the abundant, deficient and perfect rules (this is completed in figure 7, opposite):

Is there a pattern to the abundant numbers? Look at the numbers in the six times table and the numbers in the ten times table. Further exploration will reveal that all numbers in the six times table, except for 6, are abundant, but not all numbers in the 10 times table are abundant.

Pupils could explore the numbers in the times tables up to 100 to verify this.

Collate and discuss the information that the pupils have found.

Figure 6

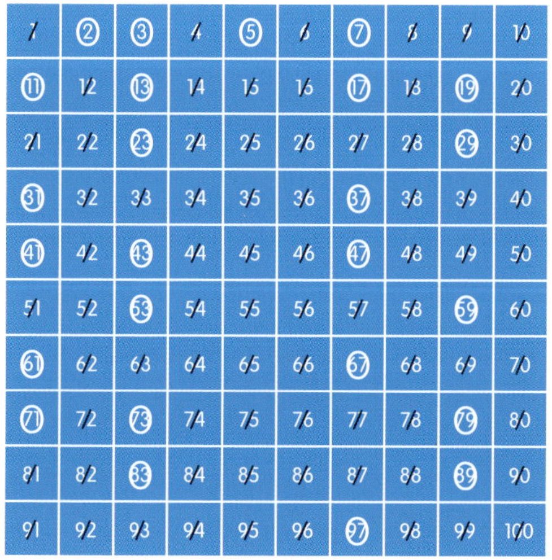
1 2 3 4 5 6 7 8 9 10
11 12 13 14 15 16 17 18 19 20
21 22 23 24 25 26 27 28 29 30
31 32 33 34 35 36 37 38 39 40
41 42 43 44 45 46 47 48 49 50
51 52 53 54 55 56 57 58 59 60
61 62 63 64 65 66 67 68 69 70
71 72 73 74 75 76 77 78 79 80
81 82 83 84 85 86 87 88 89 90
91 92 93 94 95 96 97 98 99 100

* Pupils will need access to the 'Sum and Product' Photocopy Master at the back of this booklet or available to download from the Numicon website: http://www.numicon.com/numicon_free_resources/teaching-support-resources/resources_for_numicon_activities.html

Figure 7

Number	Factors	Properties
1	1	Deficient
2	1,2	Deficient
3	1,3	Deficient
4	1,2,4	Deficient
5	1, 5	Deficient
6	1, 2, 3, 6	Perfect
7	1, 7	Deficient
8	1, 2, 4, 8	Deficient
9	1, 3, 9	Deficient
10	1, 2, 5, 10	Deficient
11	1, 11	Deficient
12	1, 2, 3, 4, 6, 12	Abundant
13	1, 13	Deficient
14	1, 2, 7, 14	Deficient
15	1, 3, 5, 15	Deficient
16	1, 2, 4, 8, 16	Deficient
17	1, 17	Deficient
18	1, 2, 3, 6, 9, 18	Abundant
19	1, 19	Deficient
20	1, 2, 4, 5, 10, 20	Abundant
21	1, 3, 7, 21	Deficient
22	1, 2, 11, 22	Deficient
23	1, 23	Deficient
24	1, 2, 3, 4, 6, 8, 12, 24	Abundant
25	1, 5, 25	Deficient
26	1, 2, 13, 26	Deficient
27	1, 3, 9, 27	Deficient
28	1, 2, 4, 7, 14, 28	Perfect
29	1, 29	Deficient
30	1, 2, 3, 5, 6, 10, 15, 30	Abundant

What Next?

This Investigation can be taken further by the most able mathematicians. Start by introducing the following:

Quaternion Identity
This states that all prime numbers can be made by adding up to four square numbers. Ask the question:

'Can you show that the quaternion identity is true for prime numbers up to 100?'

Goldbach's conjecture
This states that all even numbers greater than or equal to 4 can be made by adding pairs of prime numbers. Ask the question:

'Can you show that Goldbach's conjecture is true for all even numbers up to 100?'

Euclid
The ancient Greek mathematician Euclid, recorded the Fundamental Theorem of Arithmetic in his IX Book of The Elements. The theorem states: Every number greater than two is prime or a unique product of two or more primes. Or put another way: All numbers that are not prime can be made by multiplying prime numbers together, for example:

$6 = 2 \times 3$, $12 = 2 \times 2 \times 3$, $15 = 3 \times 5$

Ask the question:

'Can you show that the Euclid's Theorem of Arithmetic is true for non-prime numbers up to 100?'

Further investigations with Abundant, Deficient and Perfect Numbers
Did the pupils find more than two perfect numbers? Perhaps not as the next one after 28 is 496.

Perfect numbers have a direct relationship with prime numbers and powers of 2 (notice that the factors of 6 and 28 include the powers of two).

'Does this rule hold for 496'

Here are some abundant numbers:

12, 18, 20, 24, 30, 36, 40, 42, 48, 54, 56, 60, 66, 70, 72, 78, 80, 84, 88, 90, 96, 100, 102

Some of these are in the 6 times table, some are in the 10 times table, but 56 is in neither. In a group investigate 56 then ask the following questions:

'Can you use what you have learnt to find other abundant number patterns?'

'Why is 50 not abundant while 20, 30, 40, 60, 70, 80 and 90 are?'

'Is there a relationship between deficient numbers and prime numbers?'

'Is there a pattern to the abundant numbers?'

'What other connections can you see?'

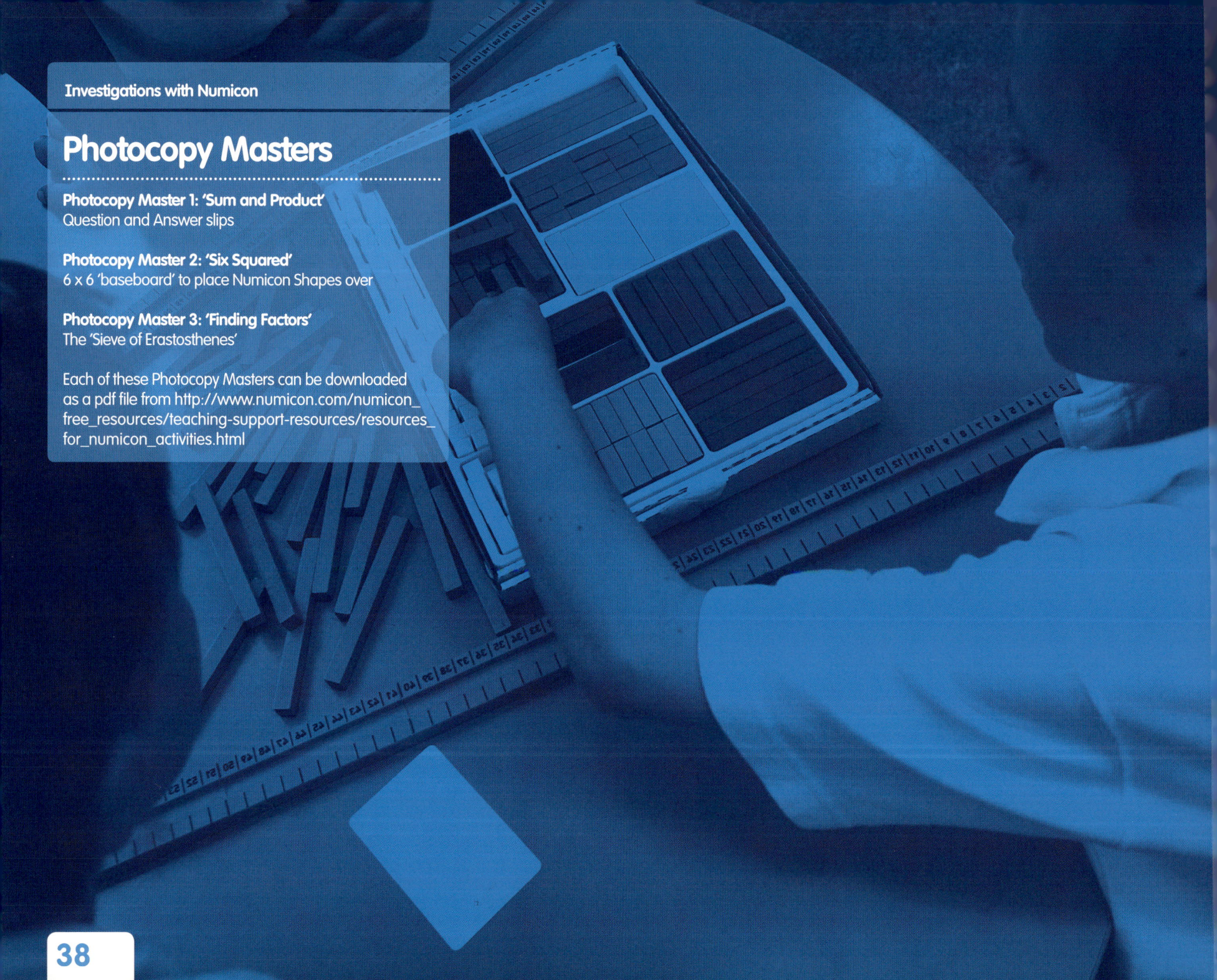

Investigations with Numicon

Photocopy Masters

Photocopy Master 1: 'Sum and Product'
Question and Answer slips

Photocopy Master 2: 'Six Squared'
6 x 6 'baseboard' to place Numicon Shapes over

Photocopy Master 3: 'Finding Factors'
The 'Sieve of Erastosthenes'

Each of these Photocopy Masters can be downloaded as a pdf file from http://www.numicon.com/numicon_free_resources/teaching-support-resources/resources_for_numicon_activities.html

Name:

Sum:

Product:

Name:

Sum:

Product:

Name:

Sum:

Product:

Name:

Sum:

Product:

Name:

Sum:

Product:

Name:

My two Numicon Shapes are:

and

Name:

My two Numicon Shapes are:

and

Name:

My two Numicon Shapes are:

and

Name:

My two Numicon Shapes are:

and

Name:

My two Numicon Shapes are:

and

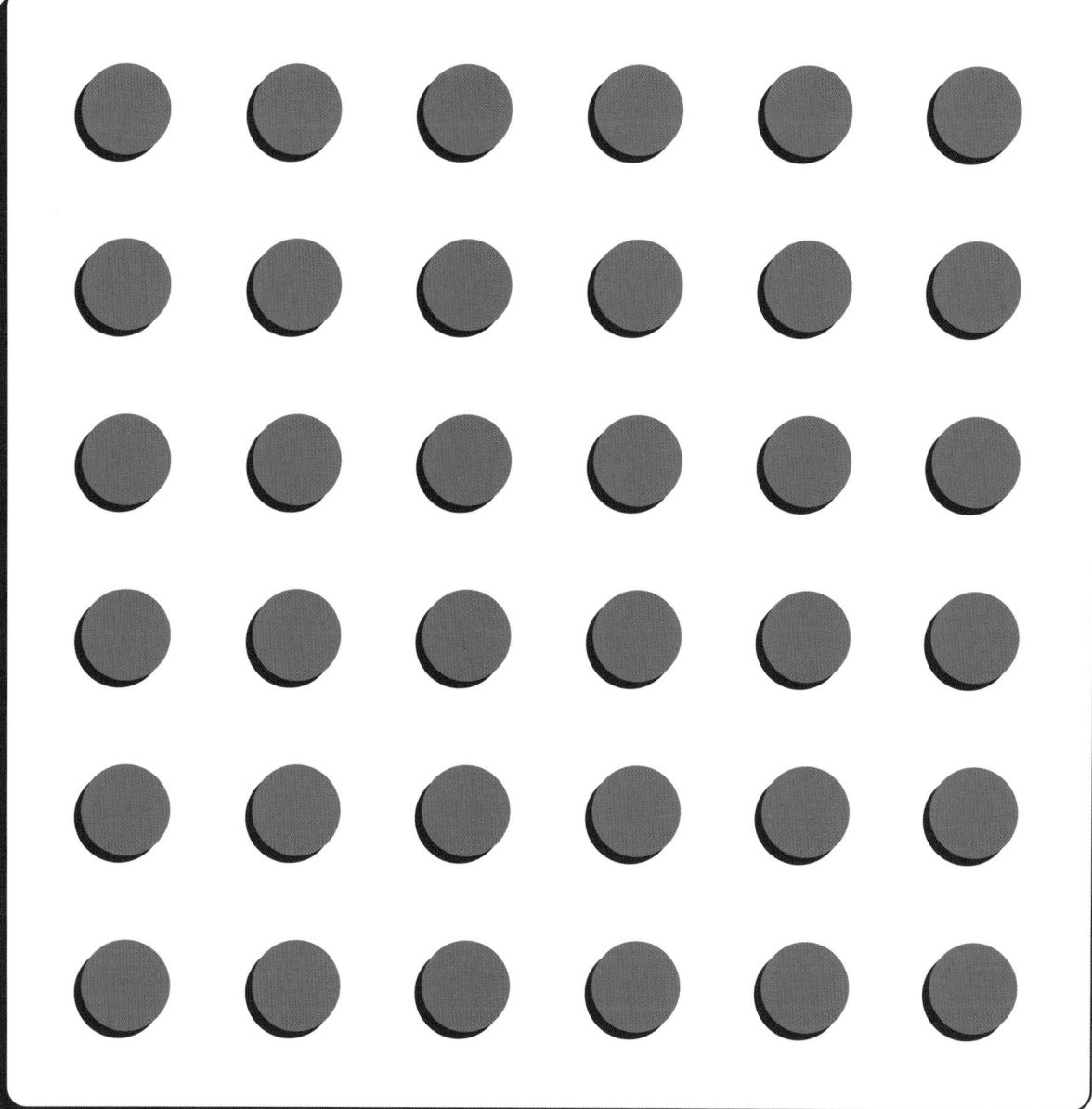

1	2	3	4	5	6	7	8	9	10
11	12	13	14	15	16	17	18	19	20
21	22	23	24	25	26	27	28	29	30
31	32	33	34	35	36	37	38	39	40
41	42	43	44	45	46	47	48	49	50
51	52	53	54	55	56	57	58	59	60
61	62	63	64	65	66	67	68	69	70
71	72	73	74	75	76	77	78	79	80
81	82	83	84	85	86	87	88	89	90
91	92	93	94	95	96	97	98	99	100